The Family Living in Warmth

DAN HOFFMAN

Leavitt Peak Press

ISBN: 978-1-957956-43-5 (sc)
ISBN: 978-1-957956-44-2 (e)

Rev. date: 09/13/2022

CHAPTER 1

Prayer Makes God Aware

Warmth is a way to live if you and the people you are with are all living each day in communication with God .

When a person prays to God, that time of talking to Him is like talking to Him through a phone call . Being able to communicate with Him whenever we want to is a true gift from God because we can talk to Him about anything .

It is also good at times not to talk or communicate with other people because it seems like too many people these days are not connecting with God, and with that truth, it is exceptionally good to talk to God and ask Him who we should have as friends .

If a person who is a Christian ever gets into good contact with other people who are not Christian, it is best to see how those people are living their lives before becoming friends with them, and that is because we do not want our lives with God to become a struggle .

A strong and full life with God, the Holy Spirit, and of course Jesus is absolutely the best form of a life that anyone can live these days . The reason for that is because we receive so much love from Them, which nobody else here can level up to .

Throughout the Bible, we can learn so much about the best ways to connect with Them . At times in the Bible, it can be hard to understand, but we are lucky to have Them, and they will help us through anything that we need . That fully includes the times when we read our Bibles because it can get confusing .

Simple prayers to Them for guidance when we read the Bible can help us to learn so much more about our Holy Family . Having all the information about Them in our minds, we can maybe help other people get to know Them, and that will make their lives so peaceful that it is hard to believe .

At times in our lives, it can seem like we are on a boat that is going through bad times with the weather . When a person gets bad weather while they are sailing, the ride can be so bouncy, and that person can also get so wet .

It is pretty much like when we are on a real boat during either of those times . When we are on a real boat or traveling on a boat during our time with God, our lives (boats) can seem to be so bouncy, but we can either use the oars or the engine, which are the prayers for what we need help with .

If our lives turn into a struggle, it is always best to continue going to church on Sundays . Church is a great place because at church, a person can make great friends there, and those relationships can last for such long periods of time .

The main relationship that everyone should be aiming for is one with God because the feeling that you always have a trustworthy person with you all the time is one of the best feelings a person can have .

There are also pastors at our churches, and that person can help everyone in such a great way to connect with God . Becoming a Christian is usually done at church, and when we do that, other people there see it happen, and it really helps us make good friends with everybody who goes there .

The warmth that God sends out every day to everybody who

is living on our world is such a caring and loving thing, which is almost like being anointed with His love .

God's love is like a big warm hug from Him, and it's better than any kind of hug that we can receive from any person here on earth . One way to think about it is like when we have the chance to suntan on the beach . When a person might do that, it is like getting a big warm hug from any other person . We must believe that when we feel that warmth we feel when we are in good communication with Him, we can also get that warmth whenever we pray to Him or ask Him questions about certain things .

We might receive the answer to those questions right away, but He also takes His time to give the answers . When He does that, it helps us out in so many ways, depending on what we are aiming for in our prayers .

Any person can pray for or about anything they want to get help from the Lord . When people are praying, it might be just for help, or it might also be for forgiveness for their sins .

Everybody, though they may not know it, is a sinner, and that is because the people who we are living with at this time do so many things that He does not like, and they don't notice that they are sinning from just learning in so many ways, which are full of sin . God always forgives any person from their sins, and He is such a caring and loving leader who made everything and everyone who is here on earth .

With His love and when we learn about His love and the way that He cares for all people, we for sure have the best carer and Father that anyone can get close to . Anyone can get close to Him, which is like living on a resort . Praying to Him every day is one of the best things a person can do to keep their relationship with Him solid and obeying .

There are so many other religions around this world, and the sad thing is that so many people chose one of those other religions, but none of them can get close to the leader whom we are following these days .

We all think that we are lucky to have radio stations to listen to and television to watch and relax to, but the true majority of what we get off either of those is truly secular and not the way that He wants us to hear or look at ways of life . There are always spots on the radio that we can continue our good communication with God, but it is hard to say what their radio stations are like in other countries .

What we can see on television can be so violent or secular, it is extremely hard to ever find something that has anything truthful about Christianity, except for Sundays because on that day . there are a lot of shows that are like church services . Not all are good to watch, and that is because those ones are not doing their "services" in the way that God wants them to .

The best way, though, to learn more about God is to go to church on Sundays and to maybe get into a Bible study group . While at the church, talk to the pastor about maybe living your life in the way that God wants us to . God has made the options of different churches available to us, and we should choose one that always tells truthful things .

Residing in the calm and peaceful way that God runs the earth is particularly good for a person's life . The reason for that is because He is a very peaceful Lord, and He helps whenever we need that help, and our lives turn out to be so much more peaceful and calmer than they usually are .

When a person is walking down the street, or driving somewhere, or shopping, or getting together with some friends to do something, they have kept their eyes open for whatever might be harmful to them or the people that they are with . The thing that causes that is the problem of people who do not obey the rules/lines that have been laid out for everyone to obey . It is called the law .

When a person obeys the law in the region that they live in, it can be peaceful, or it might lead to hard times that they have to go through . The reason for that is because the government says to obey the law, and if any person disobeys, they are going to be punished . God pretty much says the same about the rules that He has laid out for us .

Following those rules is a good way to learn all we can about God . It can be hard to follow those rules at times, but if we just keep in our minds that it is a way to have a solid relationship with God, then there is no reason for not following those rules .

For all people, sometimes during our lives, it seems like we are fighting in a battle to learn and possibly spread the Word of God to all the people who either just do not understand religion, or they have made the wrong decision about whether to believe and to just give their lives to God .

Everyone who is alive fights different forms of battle every day . Those battles could simply be just about the things we have to do at work or things that we go through at our homes . The best thing is that God is always fighting those battles with us, and He always wins those battles .

The reason that we are fighting those battles is because Satan has a way to get into everyone's life in a secretive way . When Satan does that, it is a usually a sin, so we need to ask for forgiveness for any time we might have sinned .

God is the best Leader that we have, so when we are told by Him to go somewhere or to do something in a certain way, we should follow His directions to the word; in other words, that means to follow His directions to how we think He is leading us on those days . What He tells us to do can be a bit

confusing at times, but the best thing of that circumstance is that He will help us through those times if we need His help .

God also sends one of His angels down to help us, and the reason for them to be sent to us is that God has got them to memorize the information that He wants us to receive . Since the angel coming to us has that message memorized, we are going to be helped .

But everyone knows, of course, that God knows all the info as soon as we send a prayer up to Him . It is good to have that kind of communication open to us and to be able to use it at any time we want or need to send a prayer to Him .

The times when we want or need to send a prayer to God are so good . He does not always answer our prayers right away, but sometimes He wants that prayer to be answered a day or two later, or maybe a bit longer than that . When our prayers get answered, that is a true gift from God because we might have been living our lives in a way that He does not like .

Living our lives in a way that God does not like is nothing more than a sin we are committing, but if we ask Him to forgive us for those sins, we will truly be on a ride with God as our driver . We all need to realize that any kind of a sin that we may commit is like a screw, which is pulling us away from Him . But when He gets those prayers, He brings His screwdriver and releases us from our sins . He does not just release us from our sins, but He also forgives us for our sins, so that is a particularly good thing to remember to do every day .

Sinning can hold a person back from anything in our lives . One of those reasons is because when a person gets addicted to sinning, those sin-chains can keep our minds into thinking only about doing things in that manner . The other thing that can happen are possible injuries or just the life we are living made harder . We can always pray for forgiveness for our sins, but it is hard to say how long it is going to take for our sins to be forgiven . The good thing about our sins being forgiven is that God forgives things fully, and it is easy to see that He is doing that straight out of His heart .

When a person gets forgiven for their sins or given help for matters that they must go through in their life, it is not hard to tell that we are getting a big warm hug from God . What that means is that when we are forgiven or helped by God, our sins are forgiven, or we might just be getting the help we all need to live our lives in the proper way .

After being forgiven for your sins, there is something that we can do that would help our lives and everyone in our communities as well . We can do things like we can go to the food bank and help with the things there, or we can become people who are spreading the Word of God all around the world . Really good groups to get with to do that kind of thing are the Salvation Army and Youth With A Mission (YWAM) .

The reason why it is so good to get involved with groups like that is because you would be helping other people find the way to get into God's family, and you would be showing them the place to go to for good food and clothing, which is easy to find with either the Salvation Army or with YWAM .

There are times in every city and in all countries around the world when people can tell that God is showing His love to every person on this planet . There are also other times when we can tell that Satan is getting his hand in there, causing awfully bad times for everyone .

When we are holding God's hand for direction through our life, He will always show us His love for everyone, even if we are thinking we should not be getting love or help from Him at that time .

CHAPTER 2

The Love from God Stretches around the World

It seems like every day in our lives, people hear about God's love, but the only thing is that they do not hear about how powerful that love is and how He wants that love to work . In the way that He places and sets up His love for us all around the world for everyone and everything, we can truly tell that He is fully a leader who has the best plans set for everything that He has created .

We just need to truly realize when we are receiving the love of God . We just need to keep our "body" senses open to finding out when He is blessing us with His love . At times, it can be like a "heated" love, but God gives us His love in any way He sees is best for that specific time we need it .

What we need to do, if we are new to Christianity, is to try to remember to give access to God to every part of us and everything we do, which is also a part of us .

The way to remember this is to write notes to remind us to pray to Him about this every day . Those notes, which we might write to ourselves, will fully help us in the time that we are living, and it might even help us when we die .

There are so many people in our world these days who show love every day, but the problem with some of them is that they must show that love while they are working, but when they do not work, they do not show any love anywhere .

Another way to think of God is like this: God's love is so good, but also so unpredictable that it is like getting a loving and fully caring animal to live with us every day and everywhere we go .

It is sort of like this . When we get a loving dog or cat or any other kind of animal to be with us, we can get so much love from those animals at the times when they see that we are fit for that love . It is sort of like the way that God gives out His love to all of us .

Not everyone shows love, but there are also a lot of people out there who are just completely full of hate or anger every day . That is a sad thing to say because when God looks at that aspect, He sees those people as either being born full of sins handed down by their parents, or some of those people just might have asked Satan to be their leader .

There is also a different form of love . It begins to be like the form of love that we receive from God, but after a bit of time, it starts to show some evilness in it . That is because Satan has created that form of love .

Every time Satan gets to use that evil love out there, it can do so much damage to the way we are living or in our walks with God . We work hard to keep a good and a true loving relationship with God, who is God of everything .

A lot of those people who are doing evil ways fully are following Satan in a religious manner . What those people need to realize is that if they continue to live their lives in that way, then they will truly go to hell when they die at the end of their lives .

Those people are called Satanists . There are many other religions around the world, but the only thing is that without God in them, Satan is their leader . As stated, in a way, Satan is the absolute worst leader that anyone can follow these days because of all the evilness that he puts into everyone as a curse .

All those different forms of evilness that Satan is putting into all of us is nowhere near strong enough to stop God from stopping Satan from doing that to everyone . All we need to do is do our usual praying for God's help .

God also has angels, which a lot of people have had contact with, but no one really knows anything about angels and the way that they work with us . Everything can be confusing these days, especially spiritual things, but if we seek definition for our questions about it in the Bible or by praying and asking God, we will then have a clear mind about that topic .

Please remember this . Any person, if they have access to a Bible, should read a scripture out of it every day . If all people did that, they would find that their lives would be much easier to live than usual and possibly have more friends . There are so many different "stories" in the Bible that lead us to the light of God . What happens when we read from the Bible is that a scripture will probably get sent to us from Him, and we will keep it in our minds as a reference for different forms of spiritual information .

Keeping a scripture in our minds in that way is a great thing to do because it does not just help us, but there are times that come up when we are talking to other people who might need the help from God in that manner, and we can help them by sharing to them that scripture .

Here are some of the ways to think of how God sends out His love to everybody . We all use remote controls a lot for a lot of things, and He distributes His love in that same way .

In a way, He sort of "presses buttons" to send out His love (I believe this is a good way for the kids to believe) .

Or if we are picturing vehicles in our minds, whatever kind, God can be the driver of that vehicle, which is us . So just think of it in that way . As we are living our lives as Christians, with God as our leader, we are the car for God, so we can say that He is in our lives, and with thinking of it in that way, it is much easier for everyone .

Any person can be born with any form of medical disabilities, but at any time, by His choice, God will heal those disabilities, probably by just using His love . There are numerous prayers to God that people send out to Him every day about this topic and many other more topics . He loves everyone, and He cannot hold that love back, so we are all blessed with it .

Another way to look at it is like this . When the love from God comes down upon us, it is like the mountains by the rivers or the oceans or lakes . The heated love from God makes the snow on those mountains melt . The snow right now can be thought of like all the sins and evilness in the world . We do not need to worry about that form of snow because God's love is the most powerful thing all around this planet .

You can also look at this topic this way . Think of boats on the water or in pictures, like sailboats . When you think of it like a sailboat, God is the boat, and we are the captains and the crew of the ship . We would truly just have one thing to worry about, and that is that Satan can send horrific winds that can hit the boat at any time and can do terrible things to the water, like huge waves or whirlpools . Either of them can be very damaging to the boats, or they can ruin the boat completely .

Another way to think of God is like this . He is the absolute best artist that the world has ever had in all time . I have no idea what His favorite form of art is, but no matter;

He does it all out of love . With all the different countries and communities around this world, there are so many different forms of art that can be done to show love . Anything can be done in a way to show the love of God .

A thought of God as our pieces of clothing that we wear every day is a strong thought to think . What I mean by that is this: When you are wearing your clothes, just ask God to be with you, and maybe, at that time, He will get into your clothing and hug you while you wear it all day . You will find that no matter what you are wearing at that time, you can pray to Him for that, and your life will at that time will be a bit more relaxed .

There are great medical companies and other forms of companies all around the world where God is fully working with them . Those are like the hospitals for people and the ones for animals, and there are shopping centers like malls and other similar places . There are schools too, whose focus is mainly on God, but these days, the kids are not taking that anywhere near seriously .

The malls and other shopping centers are so open that when any size of a group of people who are Christian go into it and pray for a form of help, everyone in there might get that help from God without even knowing about it . Isn't that amazing?

Calendars can also be thought of in this way . They have so many days on it per month and with empty space left in every day, so everything we want to do, those things can get written into those spaces . It is also easy to remind us of the ways in which we like to get connected with God .

We can also think of ourselves like flowers and similar plants . They all need forms of food, water, air, and places to fully grow . It can be like this: We can choose our favorite plant and be that one for God . After that occurs in our minds, if we want to be it, we just always need to keep it open in our minds to our Father because He is our loving gardener for eternity .

It can also be rather easier than any of the ways already stated in this chapter . If we just think about all the things that we have in our homes, all we need to do is place ourselves in them the same way, like how we did it with the flowers or the clothing .

A way to look at this is like this . You ask God to bless your dishes so no one will get hurt by them and only get great meals and drinks from them . Now there is also the televisions and radios, phones, paintings, other forms of art, and, you may not believe it, all cleaning materials .

All you need to do is to just keep in your mind that He is the most powerful thing in this world . That should not surprise anyone because He created the entire universe . We, as humans, are always trying to fix everything and fully find out all the information about everything in this world and out in the surrounding territories . There is one thing that we all really need to keep focused on though .

For I, the Lord your God, will hold your right hand, saying to you, "Do not be afraid . I will help you ." (Isa . 41:13)

With God saying that to all of us, it is a great thing to keep referring to because any person never wants to forget how caring and loving He is . He is always with us, guiding us to that destination where He wants us to go to .

That destination is not just heaven, but He also guides people to schools and to places where they are working and to nice living arrangements when they are retiring . The way in which He guides us is terrific . If there is any point of time during those tours when we might be needing some help, like we might be confused or under a lot of stress from the world that we live in at regular times, all that can hold us back . All we need to do is ask Him for His help through that and to show us how to cope with that stuff on our own .

There are so many ways that Satan is trying to get into every person's life these days . He easily portrays all the different forms of evil from all around the world on television . That evil even comes out from the places where we are least expecting it to come out from .

Satan can start fights in unexpected areas, like in family and friendships . The way that God stops all the evilness of Satan from occurring is sort of like this . We can think of it like when a person must take their meds . God has prescribed the entire world with His medication, and that will stop that evil from doing any more damage to what it has already done . You do not have to go to your doctor to be prescribed those meds, but at some time in your prayers, God will do that for you because He is our doctor also .

God also likes to bring us together in warm ways . Just think of God being the main player for all the teams in all the different sports these days . He is also the coach for all those different teams in those sports .

That makes living our lives, or playing those "sports," much easier to bond with God, our main team member . This is also easier to remember for a lot of us since so many of us are having extremely hard times in our lives .

We get tired, in a way, from those forms of sports, but we also get the absolute best exercise from playing any of those . The exercise that we get from those sports is spiritual . It comes to us fully as a gift from God containing His love and His thoughts and information at times .

Golf is also a sport that people can use in their minds when they are both on the same side . God will be the one hitting the ball, and that person will be the ball, and angels are the clubs and the bag . That fully makes a team, a good, pure one that is sure to win if the rules are followed .

Of course, we are playing those spiritual golf games against Satan, so it is hard to say where the holes lead the balls when the balls go into them . Is it heaven or hell that those balls are heading to once they enter those spots that God aims for in that game?

Not all people die as Christians, and pretty much all people die with sin in them, so we are all going to have to spend a bit of time in hell . What we need to do is accept that . Nobody will ever be able to go straight to heaven like Jesus could .

So if all of us just kept trying to live our lives as close as we could to the ways that Jesus lived His life, our life might be easier, and we probably would be on the road to heaven with assurance .

God is also like a banker for everybody . Everyone needs help with their bank accounts all the time . Everyone just needs to find out that He is the best banker that anyone can get in this universe .

During these times, and with all the different forms of living we are having to go through, we need to "purchase" spiritual things to help us through our lives . We also need to buy food and clothing and possible things for entertainment, in spiritual form from God, in our homes .

What we need to remember and focus on when we are feeling weak in our walks with God is this . We can always ask to go to Him in prayer and ask Him for any assistance that we might need at that time, and we can always bond more with Him at any time we may have possible .

CHAPTER 3

We Have to Come into the Cold Sometimes

Every day, we can all live with God in our lives . There is only one thing though . A lot of people forget about God and the glorious ways in which He helps everyone in their different ways . If any person is living their life without God as their Savior in it, then their life is going to be much more difficult than normal .

The coldness in our spiritual lives is brought to us by Satan . When God shows us His love, it can have a good amount of heat in it, but there are times when we are either sinning too much or when some people decide to turn away from Him . If either of those happen, then we are too far away from God to be accepted into heaven when we die .

To get out of those circumstances, what we should do is this: pray to God and ask for forgiveness for your sins, or just ask Him to accept you back into His family . When He accepts you back into His family, the gates of heaven will be open for you when you die for you to enter heaven .

At the beginning of every person's life, they have a true warm walk with God, which leads them into heaven . But in a person's early age in their life, someone, such as their parents or other members of their family, can open their minds to the evil ways in which the world seems to be living these days .

At any time in their life, after they get all that information and knowledge of those evil ways into their minds, a person, at any age, can get hit with thoughts of what to do, which are sent to them by Satan . If they can tell that it is not the right way that they should be going at that time, then all they need to do is ask God for guidance to get through those times of heaviness sent by Satan .

Some people might treat you like a child throughout your life, but do not start thinking that you are an actual child . In those days, what you need to do is something like this . Think of how your days of living are going right now, and then compare those thoughts to similar thoughts of how your days were back when you were an actual child .

Usually, children are full of the warmth of God, but the only thing is that with the influence of Satan being in everyone's life, we need to try hard to keep our children, at any age, pure and fully focused on God .

There are times when we are praying and getting prayed for when we might feel the warmth of God's love throughout our entire body, and it is hard to say what that is representing from God and maybe we think, "Is Satan faking that?"

That is the way Satan works . He either works in very real and painful ways, or he may be faking it, but those ones would still be very painful to everyone . If a person does not go to God, asking for help in that situation, that pain, which was given to us from Satan, can last through our entire lives in very painful ways .

Going to God into any situation, especially the ones that we will have with Satan, will have God fighting for us to get Satan and all that evil away from us . In any situation like that, going to God for His assistance should be an easy thing to remember .

Not everyone these days believe all the information about the goodness that God is offering us or the horrid, evil situations that Satan puts us into . It is hard to understand all the different levels of information that can turn out to run our lives in whatever way we let them .

Out of the different forms of entertainment these days, it is rather hard in certain places to find entertainment based on Christianity . There are so many television programs, movies to watch, music to listen to, clubs and similar places like that to go to, which usually show nothing Christian in them . At times, there are Christian radio stations, and sometimes there might be Christian shows . Do not worry, there is always a lot of Christian music around the world .

We can always make our own forms of entertainment as well . The main one is in all of them, where we are getting into good discussions with the other people who we might be playing games with, or maybe just having a coffee with that group of them .

Anyone else is good to talk to about God and His ways of showing His love to the whole world . Other ways to think of God are like this . He is like a doctor with the way that He heals us when we pray for that, or we can think of Him as the leader of our government where He is supposed to have complete control over our lives .

When we are with God and any of His family here on earth, we are truly in His warmth of love and blessings, which He decides to bless us with every day . His blessings can be of any kind, and that is because the Lord has so many people following Him down here that He knows all the current information that He uses in those blessings .

Even a person who is not a Christian can be blessed by God if He sees that they are proper for that . Everybody thinks that they are going to get the blessing that they ask for as soon as they ask the Lord for it, but everyone needs to realize that it all really comes to us in God's timing .

The proper thing to do to receive a blessing from God, which will probably warm us up in those cold areas we have been going, is this . What we should do is see if we can get other people in our churches to pray for us for that same reason .

After we get any form of a blessing from Him, we have to thank Him fully, and we do that because if we did not have God, then none of those things would ever become true . Some of the prayers that we make also might not happen right away, but God decides on the time when that prayer is going to come true .

All in all, this world is like winter all year round . To get into a warmer part of the year, what we need to do is combine with the ways of God and everything that He has laid out for us in Christianity . With doing that, it will be like dressing up in warm clothing for winter or any other time of the year we do not like .

I do not mean actual clothing because those outfits are going to be spiritual, which are obviously going to be the most expensive . Nobody will be able to see those outfits, not even us, but the thing is that whosoever receives one of them, they are going to fully feel the warmth and possible healing from God .

People lie so much about anything, and of course, that is a sin . It is just that we need to also try to keep all the details that we might learn in our lives to help keep us away from sin . To stay away from sin, what we need to do, again, is to focus on God's teachings and also live our lives as fully as we can by

His rules . The sinning that we all might do in our days put us deeper into the cold area, but of course, nobody wants to be in there, where Satan is putting all his plans into action . Of course, with all that evil being in working motion all the time, we need to be careful when we are doing anything on any day .

Thoughts can also be a sin, so we need to watch what we are thinking about . It is much better just to keep thinking about good things, both in what God has laid out for us in the Bible and just ones that we might be able to pick out from the huge selection of thoughts that any human is given in a day .

A person can also pray and ask God to just give them clean thoughts for the rest of the day, or even longer, and if He does not want the person to work on it, He will bless them with that chain of good thoughts before they even ask for them . Having a day full of pure thoughts is something that people all around the world these days want . If everyone took this seriously, then more people than what you might be expecting are going to get those thoughts .

Those thoughts, which we might get from Him, could truly help us out every day that we use them . In a way of comparing of how to get those thoughts, do this . It is like charging up any batteries that we might need to use again . The company that makes those batteries is named Good Thoughts, so all that battery power is going to be a good way to think .

It is not hard to get into that battery power and to also put it into full use . What a person needs to do is to first become fully connected with the Trinity . That can be done by just asking for forgiveness for your sins, and then asking Jesus to be your Savior . With Jesus being in your life in that way, you are then open for any of your prayers to be answered .

And do not forget, you can always loan one of those batteries to anyone who you might think is really needing that battery power . Everyone who is alive needs that power, and that is because it helps a person to run in the proper way whenever they use it .

CHAPTER 4

Bring Children into God's Family

If you already know all the information that we are all the children of the Lord, then good for you, but the thing is that there are so many people who do not know about Him . They are mainly living in other countries all around the world, so that is why we need to go out and help them .

We do not always have to go out into those other countries if we are not able to; we can just strongly pray for Him to help all the people who are out there to get the Word across to them . Hopefully, once they hear about God and maybe see a miracle done around them, it might just lead those people to become Christians .

We can also do that ministry in nearby places to where we are living because that would be so much easier for transportation for anyone who is living in those areas . Spreading the Word is something that God really likes for us to do . It does not matter what age we might be; we should start getting out there at any time . When we do that, the main thing we need to remember is to treat as many as we can the same as we would friends and family .

We are tasked to open the minds of all those other people, and that is possible for us to do with God . We must also lead them toward Christianity, which is sort of a redeeming thing to do, and we have to teach those people how to do that to others as well .

Satan manages to get into this area of the Christian faith, so days can be very confusing for anyone . We have the Trinity always fighting hard against Satan, but it is good to say that the one who is going to be the winner when we go to Him in the proper way is God .

When a person of any age becomes a believer in God (you know, a Christian), then so much more peace and happiness can spread around in the area where they are able to spread it . Any of the people who have accepted God to be their leader is one of His children, and it is good for them to bond together as much as they can .

Strong Christian families and friendships are great for the world to have . They tend to keep the world cleaner than what Satan is wanting . Keeping it clean in that way is so good that the world might also get to a pure way for it to function, but it is just up to all the different kinds of leaders around our world—like in the governments and in companies and in the illegal gangs—who are making the choices on how everyone is living .

We hear about all the different things happening around the world mainly through the television, the newspapers, and the radio stations . We also probably receive the most information off the computers; you know, when a person goes online .

When anyone gets information about something that they think is bad or disturbing for that area of the world where they heard it was happening in, they can just pray to God and ask for those people in those areas to be assisted in their lives . Aiding anyone is a good thing to do if it does not bring those people to do something bad to other people around them .

These days, it is hard to say which person is telling the truth when you first meet them . For others to get to know you in a good way, you can tell the truth when you are talking to a person, and just tell the truth as much as you can . Doing that, your life should be a bit more peaceful than if you were a complete liar .

Coming home to God's family is the best thing to for anyone's life . When you think about all the things we do in our households, it is pretty much the same in description in the household, which God is offering to everyone to live in . When we are in actual heaven, after we die, I believe that we are going to be blessed with the absolute best living environment that we could ever get in the spiritual way .

God just mainly asks easy things of us, like to treat everyone else well and with respect, etc . If we do those easy things that He asks us to do every day, it will lead to a nice and strong family relationship with God . But it does not just stop at being a family relationship; it also opens to be like an extraordinarily strong friendship for our lives .

As any child, we should always like to be getting together with other Christians at a possible Bible study in our churches . Studying as much as we can about God from the Bible is a great thing to do when you want to learn more about God and build a strong relationship with Him .

The teenagers these days get the option of going to a Christian youth group at the churches they might be attending or the ones at other churches where one of their friends have invited them to go with them . Churches are everywhere, but all those churches that you might hear about may not all be Christian ones .

You need to remember about all the different religions these days, and some of those that are not Christian meet in their homes on whichever day they choose, but just keep in mind that those are led by Satan, not God .

Here is a way to think of what Satan is like . He is like a hunter, a hunter who goes out all around the world all the time to capture as many of us as he possibly can into his domination . Getting captured by Satan is something that is completely horrid for us to go through, but if we watch the way in which we are living our lives, we can probably stay out of that .

If we do get into that, then all we need to do is pray for God's help to forgive us for our sins and to maybe also clear our thoughts . God always helps with our fight against Satan because He does not want to see any of us heading into hell .

An easier way to think about this situation is in this way . We are grounded, and God, our Father, relieves us from being grounded, so we are free to go if we follow Gods' guidelines . During any part of our lives, it does not matter what age we are because we can start being a child of Gods' at an incredibly young age or even when we are already in our nineties .

It also does not matter which country we may be from because since God created the entire world, He will accept anyone from anywhere who decides to follow Him . There are lots of things to do in this world, which have been created by the men and women these days, and for an exceptionally large amount of those things, we need to ask for forgiveness for any of those things that we may have been doing that turn out to be sins .

Of course, the first thing that we should try to teach to the children in our areas is not to sin because if they stay sin- free, they are going to have a stronger connection with God . Anyone having a strong relationship with God is a wonderful thing for them to have . They can learn so much and bond so much with Him with what He has been teaching to them .

All in all, it is just your choice if you want to be one of God's children, and He is the best Father who is out there at this time and will ever be .

CHAPTER 5

Learn How to Build a Strong Relationship with God

Pray and read Bible verses every week, ones that God may tell you to read or maybe verses that you have heard in the current church service . They can help you learn a lot about God and what He is out there to do . All in all, the Lord has an excellent business running for Him, completely under His direction .

That is one way that a person can think of it, or they could just think of those situations in their original ways that we were taught when we were kids .

In our daily lives here on earth, we always need to build friendships or family relationships in strong ways . But of course, everyone should know that the better relationships we have with anyone in any way is going to make our time while we are living more peaceful, and that is what everyone wants—hopefully .

Majority of the good relationships that we are probably going to make are friendships, but we can also make some exceptionally good ones with our coworkers at our jobs .

All in all, we have a huge selection of all the different kinds of relationships that we might want to get involved in with people that we meet . The main thing is, though, try to remember to keep God involved in any relationship that you might get into, and then He will tell you what to do in those relationships .

Having a good relationship with God involved in it is a great one to have, and it can be extremely rewarding for anyone to have . What I mean by that is that in any kind of a relationship, you can always bring God into it with you . You might be the only Christian in that relationship, but if you have brought God into it with you, you can continue to pray for all your friends for whatever reason they might be needing that help from God .

Everyone fighting so much these days, like just out on the streets or in classrooms or in actual world wars, which are happening in different spots all around the world . It takes a lot of prayer to hopefully stop all those wars that are happening everywhere to be calmed down and hopefully stopped by the loving grace of God .

The main problem with all that fighting that is happening all around the world every day is that fighting is not the way that God wants us to live our lives . It can be extremely hard to find a way to be peaceful with some people because everyone is different in their opinions of how their lives should be run, and it also seems like everyone has different opinions on the way of how wars are run and things like that .

Any person could join with a group to spread the Word, groups like the Salvation Army or Youth With A Mission (YWAM) . Both groups could learn how to spread the Word around their communities or maybe to other countries around the world .

To do that, though, the main thing that the people who are involved with either of those groups just need to remember to have a strong connection with God and with their coworkers too . With having such a strong bond with God during that time, those people are going to learn so much good information about spreading the Word to others during any period of the year, and in any country on the planet too .

Building a strong relationship with God is the absolute best relationship that any person could ever find anywhere . That it is true because with God being the head leader of our family, with Him having that role, then every person who is here has the option of either following Him or choosing another way to go when they are trying to find a religion .

What we need to get across to the people we know is that the only good religion to follow is Christianity . There are so many ways that God works through anybody, and it does not really matter because people work everywhere, and if those people agree to it, then the work that God has told them to do will be done .

Some of the ways that God might work through some people are ways that are regularly thought of being from another religion . The thing is, though, that with the way that God is so loving and caring about everything, a lot of the time, those prayers that we pray have a good chance of being answered .

The way that we can be sure to have our prayers answered is by trying hard to not sin for as long as we can . We can also try to ask for healings if anyone we know needs it or if we do it personally .

Helping others is something that God is calling everyone to do, but all in all, it is just their final choice of if they are going to help those other people out or not, or if they are just going to live their lives in a sinful way . God, of course, does not want anyone living their lives in a sinful way, so He has just paved out an exceptionally good road for us to direct our lives down .

It is not really that hard to make a final decision on which way you may be wanting to live your life . The only problem with that is to keep up to the rules that you need to follow to make that decision at the end of it all .

The best decision that any human could ever make for their life, at any time, is to become a Christian . All the other religions that a person can hear about every day are just not as good for anyone as Christianity is .

The reason for that is because those religions do not focus fully on God and everything that He wants to teach to all of us . When a person is first deciding on which religion they want to be a part of, it can be rather confusing to them, and that reason is because it is not just God who is providing info but also Satan in his evil ways

CHAPTER 6

Living Life in a Peaceful Way

God wants everyone to live their lives peacefully, but the only problem is that Satan gets his thoughts and actions into people's lives at times . The way that we can avoid Satan is by praying to God and asking for His help to rid us of that evilness .

The way that we can be sure that we are going to get into a peaceful life is by asking God to accept us into His family . Well, if we also need to do a fair amount of work to get into a peaceful life, every human can follow the rules properly to assist other men and women so that they can get to know God, and then things are going to go well .

Everyone wants to live their lives in peaceful ways, not just by not fighting with other people, but also no harsh Spiritual Wars that can bring a person down in so many odd ways .

Praying to God can bring a person out of either of those forms of fighting . If you check out the Bible, you might just find out the proper ways to pray and help any other people in person .

Having God to help you get through any hard times you might be having is always good for anyone, but sometimes it can be hard to understand how He is trying to help . When a person prays for assistance, the way to sort of understand how God may be getting in there and aiding them is like this: If you need to pray in a situation like that, God might tell you to look at a certain Bible verse or maybe talk to someone else whom He has deemed qualified for that situation .

The Bible verses that He tells you to study at times are good for you . If you read those fully and then try to help as many of the people who you know who might need help from God, you might be rewarded by the Lord, but it is His decision of the way He will reward you .

Following the leadership of God leads, usually, to a peaceful way of living a life . If a person decides not to follow God, then their life is probably going to be a bit more turbulent than they would normally want it to be . That is one of the main reasons why it is good to follow God in that way .

Of course, it is always good to follow God in any way that you can; it just mainly comes down to making the choice between the ways that you can follow Him . At the time when you are worshipping Him, just do it in the most relaxing way for you .

Worshipping in the most relaxing way is so good because it just makes it easier to do wherever you might be doing it, whenever you might want to worship the Lord . You do not always have to worship the Lord out loud, but you can also do that just in your mind .

Living in a life that is full of peace is much better than living lives going through these current turbulent situations, like country wars . What I mean by country wars is all the fighting in all the cities, between the illegal things and the law, and then the wars between countries, where so many people are losing their lives .

It is not just in that form of war that people are losing their lives . We are all also in Spiritual Wars pretty much between the good and evil, God's side and the side Satan chose . The side that is offering us all the goodness and love that we desire is God's side .

Spiritual Wars are difficult to fight through, but if we are on Gods' side, then we can be sure that He is going to be our head warrior . Having God as our head warrior is so good because when He fights against Satan and his evil ways, God always wins .

With God bringing us through our troubling times that we might go through in Spiritual Wars, it may take a bit of getting used to knowing who to go to in that situation .

The best ones to go to in prayer during Spiritual Wars is either God, our head warrior, or Jesus or the Holy Spirit, and with the help of any of those three, we can be sure that we will be successfully helped in any Spiritual Wars that anyone might be going through at any time .

We do need to remember something though . All three of them—God and Jesus and the Holy Spirit—are all together in the end, so together they all make the head warrior, and that means that when we pray to any one of them, we are going to get help in that form of Holy deliverance .

Denying all that with the help of God and the other two is something important that really needs to be done when those circumstances arise .

The best way to do it is in groups, and with that strong prayer and in the group, we can say if we are under a Spiritual War at that time, then we would be in prayer with the group for that .

At church, a person can also go up to the front and get prayer for circumstances like this . As said earlier in the book, going to church on Sundays for church services is so good to do because you can learn so much about everything about Christianity and God and the rest of them .

Learning in that way is very calming and gives us all the information that we are searching for about that topic .

Kids think of the time that they spend at church to be like the time that they spend at their schools . They are hopefully learning so much at both of those places, but they can be sure that God is going to be with them no matter where they go .

Adults and teens who choose to go to church also might feel like they are back in school . If they do feel like that, it might be a bit more relaxing for them, or maybe it can help them bind a bit stronger with God, like in a friendship .

All in all, getting with God and His love and everything else that He has to offer us just gives us so much peace at the end of it all .

Living a life of any kind, even with God, we are going to go through some troubling times, but we can always get the help that we might need from God .

When we do, peace comes with that to release us from that stress and pain and anything else that Satan might have hit us with at that time . It is hard to figure out because Satan is trying his hardest to work undercover .

It does not matter if Satan is trying to work undercover with different things all around the world; God is always coming out clear with His love and peace and everything else that we can get in ways of assistance .

SATAN STARTED THE WARS

HE'S WORSE THAN BEFORE

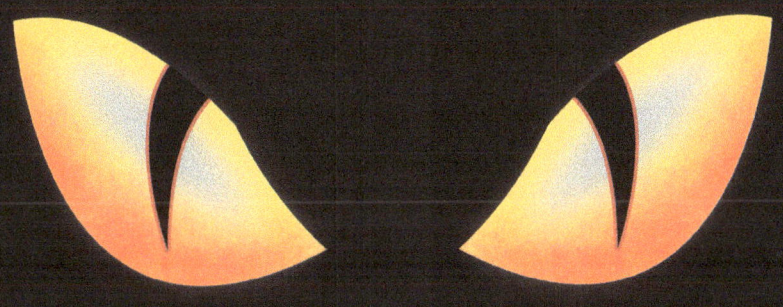

CHAPTER 1

Satan's Beginning

Satan used to be an angel in heaven . But he was a rebel and was fully wanting to take over the throne, which gives God control over everything, so when Satan started a little war up there, God kicked him out of heaven and put him into hell . With there being so many people on earth at this time, Satan has found a way to condemn the majority of the population of earth, but those of us who know that God can beat Satan in any battle keep going to God in prayer for help

in that situation .

Satan does not just get his evilness planted down in one area of the earth at a time . What he really tends to do is fill the entire world at the same time all at once, which makes it both a very hard battle to fight and also a very confusing one too .

Wars like those, which get to be so confusing and full of stress, is not to be done unless you make sure at first that you have solidified your relationship with God, which is the smartest thing to do at any time in your life .

Any types of the wars that are happening here on earth right now seem to be something that give full energy to Satan because they start with a feeling of killing other people and doing destruction, which are both evil things to do, and when we do anything evil, Satan applauds those things because of the way they represent him in his disgusting and evil ways .

There are all different kinds of wars that have been created by mankind, but Satan has made a form of a war as well, which is called Spiritual Warfare . It is a very hard one to fight, and to fully get through it, you just have to make sure that you are fighting that war on Gods' team and not on Satan's, but sadly, some people have turned and joined and become members of Satan's side .

All in all, the ultimate and truly better decision to make these days that will last you and also anyone else for all eternity is to stay away from the temptations that Satan may be trying to draw us in with because all those things are evil, and they might get us injured and just send us straight to hell .

CHAPTER 2

Fighting the War

It doesn't matter what kind of war you might happen to be fighting in anywhere in the world, it's just that you need to make sure that you keep your relationship with God sturdy and solid so Satan cannot pull you away from God at any point in your life because if that happened, there is no telling what might happen to you in both physical and spiritual ways . God is more than one thing for us . He is our King, but

He is also like our guard soldiers because He is always by our side and making sure that Satan can't attack us as long as we are asking Him to protect us in that spiritual way, which everyone needs to be .

There are a lot of different aspects to Christianity that can turn up to be quite confusing and stressful, but if we just take our time to learn as much as we can to handle on that topic, there is a definite chance that everything will turn out to be easy to understand .

God is also asking all of us who are Christian to behave ourselves during these times because with the Spiritual Wars going on, if we can stay as close as we can to God and battle Satan, there is a much higher chance that we all will defeat Satan in those wars, even though Satan never seems that he ever thinks that he might lose .

Back when we were all taking our school education, Satan even got himself into those areas, and he didn't care about what age we might be . The main thing that Satan wants to do with everyone is to get them not to focus their minds on God in any way, but to turn their heads and then go down the road that will take them into hell when they die .

It is just up to us and the personal help that we get from God to defend ourselves from Satan because that battle is tiring, and what any person might be thinking is only up to what they do to make it true or not .

The world is full of areas that are full of anger and also areas that seem to be full of love and gladness, but it really depends on which way each person who goes into those areas was raised and how they might take in those settings in the areas . Some take them seriously, and others tend to take them just as a joke .

God can get into all those areas if we pray out to Him and ask Him to help us in the ways that we might need at any particular time . God is the one that no one should ever have any doubt in because He is the absolute strongest in care and love anywhere in the universe compared to all other things .

Any Christian person at this time can join with a group like either Youth With A Mission (YWAM) or the Salvation Army to get the information about God spread to as many people as possible .

We all need to remember to go to church services on Sundays so we can learn more about God and Jesus and the Holy Spirit and have a more in-depth look into the battle with Satan and them, which includes us .

CHAPTER 3

Daily Life

There is really only one true way to live a person's life out these days, and that way is to fully follow God and His teachings that He might be giving to you because when you follow God, it just really solidifies everything about your life .

Each person needs to realize that with the way that the world is running right now, the times are getting rather stressful, and at times it can also get to be painful in physical, mental, and also spiritual ways .

God helps us greatly to get out of the stress and the pains, so He is like a doctor for everyone . Having God being here with us and aiding us in any situation we might be going through is just a way to know fully that God is truly here with us and coming through to everything that He stated in the Bible because we then actually do realize that everything coming from Him is true .

Also, a lot of the violence that people can see at any time can be on the streets or on their televisions, in movie theaters, or if they go to a play with a fair amount of violence in the script . In the world right now, it is hard to tell which way things are going for the world, like if the world is ever going to be peaceful or just continue to be a large warzone There are also countless amounts of different races and colors that people might be these days, and unfortunately, there are gangs, like the KKK, who believe in only people who have the same skin color as they do, and they go around making their ideas heard loudly .

That way for people to be acting is fully a way that God does not want anyone to be acting; it just really shows how Satan can get into people's minds and mess them up severely .

There are other types of rebelling gangs, but they might not be against race . They might be against their government or other things . It's like a buffet table that everyone can choose from to make their selection from of what to hate and rebel against .

If we just keep praying hard that all those gangs get stopped in the way God wants them to be stopped, then we will see a bit more peace in our cities, which will definitely be good for everyone at this time .

A peaceful life is something that every person wants to have, but it really just depends on who they decide to follow, either God or Satan, and God is the only one who gives out the peace in that form while Satan is pure evil .

There are homeless people these days who are living on the streets and are using containers to ask people who walk by them for some support or money . A lot of people who are faced with that question usually don't give money because a lot of the street people use that money not just for food, but also for illegal drugs and cigarettes .

We really need to support them and pray for them . A good way to help all the people who are poor is by getting with the Salvation Army and by volunteering to do work with them whenever you are able to .

CHAPTER 4

Living with Discernment

We also need to keep our eyes and our minds open in our churches about the information, maybe, that is getting portrayed about the world and just making sure that it is all truthful because there should really be no lies told in God's house .

To stay connected with God and to keep our minds open for God's information to enter it wherever we might be, we need to remember to just mainly focus on God and the path that He has laid out for us to live .

Start spreading out this information to the little kids who are around seven or eight years old, and then continue it to anyone over those ages . This can get into the elderly ages because everyone has their doubts about pretty much everything these days, and it just takes a lot of convincing, but we don't need to worry because we have God helping us with that situation .

No matter what kind of a situation might arise in your life, try hard to keep yourself focused on God and everything that He may be asking you to do if you have heard or felt in a drawing term that will bring you closer toward Him so you will understand His calls clearer .

If you think to a time back when you were younger, if you were a Christian then, think of how God helped you or maybe any other people you knew during those times . That should prove to you that God is real and full of love and that He cares for all of us, and He also is definitely something that the entire world should know fully about every day so there is less chance of a lot of people going into hell, and a higher percentage of people will be going to heaven .

God even still loves the people who have chosen to worship Satan and formed a group called Satanists . Those people say that they hate God and have ways to confuse Him, but what they don't know is that it's not true because Satan does not have that kind of power .

There is the final book in the Bible that has been named the book of Revelation, and in that book, it talks fully about how when God sets His foot on earth, all who are in His family will be taken automatically up into heaven with Him . A lot of us, though, are just going to have to go through a very troubling time because Satan is going to have control over the world for a period of time, and it's just up to each person to make their own personal decision of which way they are going to go, either follow God and go to heaven, or follow Satan and go to hell . Which sounds better to you?

THE
WARS THAT WE ARE IN
THESE DAYS

CHAPTER 1

All These Different Fights and Wars

There are so much different kinds of fighting going on in our cities these days . There is no specific topic for all the fighting, but any form of those wars in our cities or the illegal things also happening in our cities, the police are mainly handling them .

People go through all sorts of different fights and even wars, which just might be between people, countries, medical reasons, or spiritual reasons . Everyone knows what to do for the basics of the normal wars, but when it is a Spiritual War, you should just be praying a lot over that certain situation to make your walk with God a bit calmer .

Very truly I tell you, whoever believes in me will do the works I have been doing, and they will do even greater things than these, because I am going to the Father .

John 14:12

We make the final choice of whether we are going to work in own communities by spreading the Word of God, which puts us into a Spiritual War in a way, but with praying to God while we are doing that and focusing mainly on doing what He has called us to do on that day can make our day a bit easier .

With all these Spiritual Wars going on in everybody's lives these days, things can be rather confusing to figure out . Satan is the one who leads the warriors on the evil side of the Spiritual Warfare, and he is just doing all these evil things to get as many as he can to turn away from God and to head for hell when they die .

Nobody really wants to go to hell when they die, but the problem is that a lot of people do not realize that heaven and hell are actual or real places that we are going to be going to one day, but it just depends on the way in which we live our lives to determine which place we will go to .

Nobody really wants to spend eternity in hell, and so many others just do not understand the truth about God and the way to get to heaven with Him . That is why, I believe, God is calling so many of us to get out into whatever parts of the world and tell them all about God and everything that He does for us at all times .

When people hear information like that, there are a lot of people these days who think it is fake, but we should not let that bring us down because we know it is the truth . Nothing can make that truth go away because it is all coming from God, and He has the power to do anything He wants since He is the world's creator .

God will let anybody know what He wants them to do that day or maybe for the rest of their life . It is fully up to each person to make the proper final decision of what to do, according to Him, like are they going to do some volunteer work, or are they going to give some money that day, or are they going to become a missionary to spread the Word of God?

Being a missionary and spreading the Word of God is a great and relaxing thing to do, and on top of that, it also helps out everyone whom the Word gets told to . Telling that information to as many people in the world as you can is a true calling from

God, and it can be used, in a way, to fight all the bad, evil things that Satan is trying hard every day to put into our lives .

A lot of people think to live their regular lives every day, and the main thing that they do not realize or ever think about is that we are all always going through something bad in our lives . We may be getting into fights with people who live close by, or fighting with others in our family, or fighting with our friends, but there is always the path that God has made for the world to follow, which takes us out of any kind of sin or pain or confusion .

There is still another war that is being fought all around the world every day, which is a Spiritual War, where God is fighting in a very intense way against Satan and all the evil things he has created on earth and in all our lives . We just need to get the message out, saying that nothing and nobody can ever defeat God because He is so pure .

We are all fighting in the Spiritual War too . The thing about this is that all people, at any age, are fighting in this war because with the way that Satan is always getting into people's lives . He gets into everyone's lives and does all different sorts of things that are completely evil .

What we really need to do is to get the information about God spread around our cities as much as we can . Maybe we can join up a group in our church that is focused on spreading the Word of God and also possibly helping out the needy people as much as we can .

What everyone needs to realize is that even if you do not really believe that you may have sinned in that day, you should always ask God for forgiveness for any sins that you might have done . Doing that is like taking a shower because sins make us look dirty in front of God . It is always better to be clean as much as possible, but the thing is, it is up to us to do that .

Every day, we are all fighting Satan in those Spiritual Wars, but if we focus on our relationship with God, then there is a much higher chance that we are going to win any Spiritual War we might get involved in .

CHAPTER 2

The Wars Going on Around the World

We have those worldwide wars where a lot of people are dying, and there are lots of smaller wars happening in cities and towns caused by groups doing illegal things . The largest number of wars come from in between family members because everyone has their own way of arguing about things they are probably having a hard time with .

And of course, we all have to put up with Spiritual Wars happening in our lives . The more we study the information God is giving to all of us, the more informed we will be for any times when we might get into a Spiritual War .

The wars that are happening all around the world these days seem to be more real than the Spiritual Wars . There are ones where people fight other people, causing blood to bleed and people to die . Fighting is not the way to live a life . We all should actually be showing our love and care to everyone else, pretty much the same way that God shows His love and care to everyone on earth .

The teachers in public schools, grades 1–12, are not allowed to teach anything that includes the information of Christianity . Then it is fully up to the parents of the children to teach them at home about God and tell them Bible stories when they are going to bed .

It may seem like kids have easy lives to live these days, but people just do not realize that there is a lot of bad stuff happening in every kind of school, like illegal drugs, and there are times when the kids get into fights . The teachers in the schools are hopefully good enough to teach the kids the proper way that they should be behaving and doing any kind of work they might get involved with .

It is hard to say, when walking down a busy street, who might be carrying a gun or some other weapon on them . The reason why it is so difficult is because there are a lot of people these days who pickpocket people as they walk by them, and others hold up stores for a large amount of money . Those people who do that stuff should be made to serve time in jail or something like that, depending on age .

Those people might have been led to do that kind of stuff from television shows or movies or even what they might learn in classes at the schools in whatever level of teaching they are giving in those schools .

Raising children of any age is difficult to do these days because there are all the things brought on by the Spiritual Wars, and not everyone is 100 percent normal . A lot of people have disabilities these days . They might have problems with their muscles, and some other people have mental disabilities . There are lots of other disabilities to add to those, like those that need medication, like epilepsy or diabetes . It is pretty much a war, but it is one that God is helping us to win . People, when they are out shopping with family and friends, can easily get into fights about prices or what to purchase . Everyone just needs to see that they have to stop themselves from getting into any fights with anyone else about anything because that is not the way God wants us to live our lives .

Fights with anyone can lead to people being hurt and sometimes friendships being lost . If some people are fighting too much, then those people might get a divorce, but it just fully depends on their communication with each other .

With the way that some people communicate with other people, it is very easy to say that they have a hard time making friends with other people . We all just need to remember the guidelines given by God .

There are also all the different wars and fights going on in all the businesses that we all use pretty much every day . The wars and fights could be between the prices of things or if that company is allowed to sell at that current time .

Those fights or maybe wars that we might have gotten into while working our shift hours one day could lead to a Spiritual War because there is no specific place where those could happen . It just depends on how active Satan is at that time .

It just seems like so many people right now all around the world are being hurt by the evilness that Satan is hitting everyone with, but we are all blessed to have the help from God to get rid of that evil and just be purer than that .

CHAPTER 3

Groups That Help to Stop a War

There are two strong Christian groups, the Salvation Army and Youth With A Mission (YWAM), and they both do a lot of work in the way of spreading the Word of God and also helping out people who are needing any kind of help .

With YWAM, a person can get enrolled for a missionary course at a number of locations of bases . The course is five months long, two months for taking the class and then three months on an outreach spreading the Word of God somewhere in the world .

When I was young and my parents were doing the YWAM course, on their outreach, we went to Thailand and Malaysia . The people over there really do not believe in God . They have another religion, and they all believe in that strongly . We managed to help a large amount of people in those areas become Christians, and one of the first things they said was that they were never going to give up on God .

In places like those, there is always a form of a war going on between the religions . There is more than two in those countries, but some of them do not agree with each other, and none of them get along with Christianity .

So with the way that there is all that religious fighting happening every day, the only way that that can be stopped is by praying to God and asking for whatever help you might need in that circumstance at that time .

We all also have little gangs that get together every week for things like Bible study, and some get together at cafés just so they can get into good conversations .

Even after God helps us through these hard times, we all are going to have to really keep the main thing targeted in our minds so we can be sure, in a way, that we are going to accomplish the "jobs" that God has laid out for us to do .

Doing those jobs is a nice and relaxing thing to do, and on top of that, it helps those other people so much . It is just nice to know how much we might be helping them . With the Salvation Army, we can raise money to help people for food and clothing, etc . The Salvation Army also has places in cities where people can donate food or clothing or their time to help the needy, poor people .

With both the Salvation Army and YWAM fighting hard against all these different forms of Spiritual Wars, what we need to do is to make sure that we are on God's side of the battle and that we also are fully ready to fight in any parts of the wars that may come up in our lives .

Fighting those Spiritual Wars is a way to build a person's relationship with God stronger and also to give that person more information on that specific topic . With regard to topics, there is a countless amount regarding Spiritual Warfare .

There is also, of course, the police everywhere to help with all the crimes and wars going on in the cities these days caused by the gangs doing a lot of illegal things, and they kill people too .

Some kids, teenagers, and adults go around areas at night sometimes and do things like spray-painting walls, or maybe the side of a house, or something like digging big holes in people's lawns . Those people either just do not realize how that is not the way God wants us to live our lives or that He just wants us to stay safe and close to Him .

People of all ages doing those things should know this is not good for people of whatever age who are trying to figure out what to do with their life at that current time .

In our lifetime, when we have things that come up that might mess up our days, it can get to be very confusing, like a war . Kids can get to be confused in school, and adults also get into confusing parts of each day at work because of new things in store or new people to make appointments with .

But all in all, volunteering with either of those two groups, YWAM or the Salvation Army, is a really helpful thing to do for the community you may live in . If you help out with the groups that help numerous amounts of people every day, doing that brings a bit more peace into everyone's life .

CHAPTER 4

Always Fighting a Spiritual War

Spiritual War might sound like something that Satan would have started, but it is hard to say if he did or if we started it because a lot of us are in a bit of a war with God due to our sins .

There are a lot of people out there right now with different thoughts on the Spiritual Warfare and the ways to properly get it under control . The best and quickest way to get it under control is praying to God about it and fully following what He tells you to do .

You might think that children do not get attacked by these Spiritual Wars, but actually, young kids might get hit by something on the evil side, but with a large number of families being Christian these days, those kids will probably get prayed for .

When the kids might get hit by that evil, it might happen to them when they are sleeping, so they will have some kind of a different spiritual dream . The kids might call them nightmares .

Every day we might get into Spiritual Wars . It is hard to say how many might happen, if any, and also it is hard at times to figure out if we caused them to happen or if they came directly from Satan .

The main thing we need to remember in this situation is that Satan is always on our backs, trying to pull us down and away from all things God wants us to do . But we also need to keep in our minds that God is always with us and that He will help through anything that may come up between us and Satan .

There are also all those people out there these days who are Satanists . That means that they worship Satan and all the evil things he does all around the world every day . We need to make sure that we take precautions so that we have the help we will need from God in this situation to hopefully stop Satanists from doing too much bad stuff in our neighborhoods and even all throughout the cities in spiritual ways .

The Satanic people sometimes also do damage around the areas where they happen to be located, and they do it so secretly that no one manages to notice that they are the ones who did that damage .

Those fights, which include Satan in any way, are definitely all a part of the Spiritual Wars, but with God, Jesus, and the Holy Spirit on our side, we are going to win those battles . It is just going to take some concentration when they start up . We just need to pray and then focus on living in the proper manner .

Praying to any of the three of them—God or Jesus or the Holy Spirit—is like a solid link on a cell phone . There IS sometimes an occasion where we have some sort of problem getting our prayers over to them, but one way to make sure that never happens is to ask for sin forgiveness at the beginning of every time we might pray .

One thing that would be really good for all of us to do as much as we can is to pray that those other religions become much smaller or even stop their practice . There is just a countless number of different religions all around the world .

All those different religions, including Christianity, are at a form of war with each other . The thing with the religions that are not Christianity, they may say that they are worshipping something else, but they need to realize that they are actually worshipping Satan .

A lot of us do not even think about Satan or Spiritual War these days, but to get through our days fully and easily in that manner, we need to stay focused on God and the duties He wants us to do .

Even when we are doing those duties God gave to us, Satan still brings up those Spiritual Wars in our lives, and they can really make our lives harder to live . We can get through that, though, with prayer and keeping on the proper line that God wants us to walk during our lives .

Getting into prayer groups to handle any Spiritual War problems we might have or any other kind of problems as well, it is always better to have more than just one person praying for something that we need help from God for because then we can be surer that He is going to come through and help us in one of His ways .

CHAPTER 5

Fighting between Businesses

There are so many different businesses located in every country all around the world, and everyone who is working with or for those companies are in a form of a war with all the other companies in this world .

All in all, it adds up to millions of different companies selling things in as many places as possible . The reason why it can be called a war is because a lot of the time, businesses just do not seem to get along with each other, so they get into fights, and they settle them with sales or bringing in a product the other store does not have .

The main businesses that fight all the time that we need to stay aware of is our governments . The governments and certain people who are in them just keep fighting with each other . At times it can lead to countries going to wars against each other, and it is sad to say that some people actually like it when that happens .

Even when those forms of fights may seem to be over, people who either were involved in them or heard of them might spread around some information about them that is not true . Fights in our governments always use information that they might come up with, but at times, that info is not full true, and that, obviously, is not a way to keep the world in a peaceful manner of living .

The wars between countries can go on for such a long time . It is actually hard to say how long the war might be for because there are thousands of men and women for each country fighting in those wars with just a hope at the beginning of them to say which country is going to win .

Any type of war, except for Spiritual War, are ones that no one should really be fighting in because God sees them as evil . The majority of those wars cause blood to be shed and also a lot of people to die . God does not like that; it says in the Bible that we are not supposed to kill each other for any reason, but there are so many people in the world right now who just are mainly focused on living their lives in secretive and illegal ways, and for a lot of them, it contains committing murder in their life .

The ones who are secretive are the men or women who might be hired to kill someone or to sell illegal drugs or to do something similar like that . What we need to realize is that doing those kinds of things is a heavy sin, so we need to make sure we do not do that kind of stuff at any time in our life .

Staying away from anything illegal or that which causes bloodshed is definitely a better way to live a life than by following the ways of the ones that will just add up to sin .

With the way that we have all that horrid stuff happening in our cities, we have the police to help us stop those groups who are causing all those illegal things from happening to us . With the help from the police, our lives can be a bit easier to live, but hopefully, we will not have to rely on the police that much because having a lot of that kind of bad stuff in our lives can really make our lives hard to live .

Everybody's lives are hard to live because of all the things that come up between people and businesses and countries, but there is one main thing to focus on for help in that situation, and it is God . God helps us to get through any hard times we may be in, and all we need to do is to pray to God and ask for His assistance .

So many people out there do not know the full information about God, but we can spread the Word to as many as we want when we get into conversations with any other people . Telling people about God can turn out to be so helpful for a lot of those other people, so informing more people about God is definitely something that we should do as much as we can .

CHAPTER 6

Fighting Our Way into Heaven

Many people believe that as soon as they become a Christian, they have a reserved spot in heaven, but the truth is that we need to live by God's rules, which sort of pave the road for us to drive into heaven when we die, and those rules are mainly easy to follow, but at times things can come up in our lives, and they make our aim to follow God's rules difficult .

With all these difficult circumstances happening all over the world right now, we need to keep focused on living our lives in the manner that God has told us to because not living by His way usually adds up to a lot of sinning, and God does not like that . Sins can actually keep us out of heaven .

You evildoers frustrate the plans of the poor, but the Lord is their refuge .

(Ps . 14:6)

In this verse, we are told, in a way, how all the sinning we do every day just does not measure up to what God wants . God wants us to be without sin, and He will forgive us for our sins, but we are the ones who need to remember to pray for that forgiveness . After we get forgiven, we have a better chance at getting into heaven if we are Christian also .

We have so many of those evildoers in our neighborhoods these days, so we really need to keep our eyes open for anything bad or evil that might be happening in the areas around us . With all those problems being caused by those evildoers, we really have to find a way to keep our lives aimed at the spots where God wants us to go .

With staying aimed at those certain spots God wants us to go, we should be staying more stable in our walk with God because in a spiritual way, He is going to be holding our hand while we are walking with Him wherever we might go .

God's hand is the best thing to hold on to because with that, He leads us to whichever destination we are trying to get to, and it seems like in the palm of His hands, He also has a lot of information for us to use during any time of our life and also info to spread to others .

We do not just have to fight our way into heaven, but we also have to fight a bit of a battle to become Christians and to continue as Christians for the rest of our lives . God will show us the way to fight that though .

To become a Christian, what a person needs to do is ask forgiveness for their sins and then ask for Jesus to be their Savior . The reason why Jesus is the Savior is because of how He was crucified and rose from the dead after being dead for three days .

Living any part of our lives is like driving a vehicle . A way to think of it is like this: With God guiding us, it is sort of like as if He was driving our vehicle and taking us to where He wants us to go . There are other times where we have to do something with a group of people, so it would be like riding on a bus .

Of course, with us living our lives every day, something might happen to make the rides in our "cars," where we are riding with God, turn into a car accident . We do not have much to fear because God is our 911, and He never lets us down .

One of the main ways to make sure that we get into heaven is just by doing a close study on what we believe God wants us to learn . The way to find out what to study is to pray or to ask questions at church .

We can also ask God those questions we need answers to, and He might just answer those questions in your prayers, or He might select a person to give you the answers to those questions . It can be a bit confusing at times, but if we just keep the idea of getting the full information, all we really need to do after we pray is keep our minds open for His answers .

Having a good communication link like that with God at any time is really good for anyone to have in their life . Having that link is pretty much like linking arms with God and having Him lead us on the way He wants us to proceed .

We can be sure that wherever He takes us or whatever He may tell us or help us with is all done out of love . After He does something, it is not hard to tell if God used His love in that matter, but He is just the most loving one whom anyone on earth has ever heard of .

All the fights that we all have to go through every day, most of them are Spiritual Wars, other ones are world wars, but God helps us to get through all of them . There are the fights on the side of the road, fights on computers or phones, fights on the road and in the air and also in the ocean and fights at work . We just need to rely on God and go to Him if we need His help in any of those circumstances .

Here on earth, we are always having to fight our way to everything we need to do, but the best thing to use in any of those fights is what we have been taught by God .

The side we are battling against in these wars and fights is fully led by Satan, but with God being on our side, we have a very good chance of winning those fights each time . A lot of the time, we might also be fighting a form of a small battle against ourselves, considering all the ideas and thoughts we might get from TV or radio or conversations with other people .

Winning those battles and wars with God on our side will truly get us a ticket that will take us into heaven for a longtime break from what is happening here on earth .

CHAPTER 7

All the Battles, What a Rattle

We all get involved in so many different fights and wars and battles in a day, but can we say that those are being done physically or spiritually? Those things are being done in both of those ways, but even though they are being done in both of those ways, for both of them, we need God with us to help us win our fights and battles .

We are not just fighting other people, but a lot of the time we are fighting Satan and his demons when he sends them out . God is superior to Satan, but with the way that a lot of people live their lives, especially the Satanists, there is a very strong Spiritual War going on between God and Satan, and I am happy to say that I am on God's side of that war .

To fight in that battle against Satan and to be on God's side while fighting, what we should do is a lot of praying and also go to church services on Sundays when we are able to . Sometimes Satan might even try to get a response into our prayer when we get the response from God . That may sound like something that is not believable, but it can actually happen . To have it not happen, ask for forgiveness of your sins first because it says in the Bible that Satan can't do anything in clean areas, and if we are being cleansed of our sins, we can probably pray to God on a one-on-one basis .

With a person having all these different kinds of fights and battles and wars in their life, it can really shake and rattle up their life . The kinds that cause us to wear out the most are the ones that are Spiritual . The reason for that is because we have not been fully trained for Spiritual Wars and similar fights to that, but we can get somewhat trained at church .

After we do get better trained to defeat those battles, we can talk with God and plan out what we are going to do when the next time comes up that we need to fight hard against Satan and all his ways .

A way to think of Satan is like this: He is like all the dirt in our homes that we have to clean up every day . So I guess I can say that I am allergic to Satan and everything that he causes in our lives .

There are a lot of other people out there who are sort of allergic to Satan and what he does, but there also is a rather large number of people who aren't and do his ways every day . These people just need to fully understand the information about God in the proper way or to accept it to get away from Satan .

Since there is such a variety of all those different religions these days, the main thing to keep focused on when the thought of them might come up in your mind is that all the religions, except for Christianity, have been started by the hands of Satan .

Since we are all in some sort of a battle or war every day, usually spiritual, we can always go to God for the help in the fighting that we are doing at those times to come out as winners against Satan .

To make sure that we come out as winners against Satan, we need to stay in prayer with God on that topic, asking for His help in the way that He may see fit to distribute His help to us at that time .

CHAPTER 8

Spiritual War for the Poor

Who do you think are the ones who have the most need for spiritual stability with God? While they or anyone else is trying to accomplish that, there is no doubt that it is going to be a strenuous time .

The ones out of us all who are in very deep need for spiritual stability with God are the poor and also the people who may just have their lives focused on a different direction to a different religion .

Everyone may imagine that there are places to go to that have no poor/needy people in those places, but everyone needs to realize that the poor and needy people are located worldwide .

So with those people being located in all those different areas, we really need to aim to get out and spread the Word out as strongly as we can .

The type of war that the poor and needy people are really going through every day, just like everybody else, are the Spiritual Wars against Satan and all the evil things that he has planned out to happen against us .

The majority of us, though, are fighting on God's side of this battle when it is happening in our lives .

The main points of information that we need to get out about that topic are the ones about God and also the loving ways in which He is spreading His love with everyone on earth at all times, every day .

We are involved in that spreading of His love, and since we are included in that spread, that is something we should be proud of since we are included in the way that God gets that done .

A person cannot just be poor on money or food or other similar things like clothing, but anyone can be poor on their relationship with God, but that can always be rebuilt if they just target their mind to achieving a strong and solid relationship with God, which is like a friendship and also like a family relationship .

Spiritual wars can be confusing for any person, and they can also make things happen in people's lives . The best and easiest way to get through those wars are to stay close to God and to remember that you can go to Him for His assistance when those wars may come up in your life . Nobody can ever tell when Satan is going to attack, but we have God fighting with us so we will win .

It actually doesn't matter what age you might be or what race or anything because everyone is perfectly equal to each other, but a lot of people don't believe that . God loves everyone, but not all people are going to heaven when they die because you have to be a Christian to go to heaven .

So I guess we can definitely say that there is a definite Spiritual War going on all around the world right now, but God's army is going to win that war next to Satan's little army .

GOD IS THE LIGHT, LET'S STOP THE FIGHT

CHAPTER 1

The Fight Can Block the Light

There is always a fight going on between God and Satan, and that fight only has an effect on any person when they are sinning too much and trying to figure out which way would be the best way for them to follow through their life .

Obviously, everyone is meant to follow God, but still there are so many people who decide to follow in the true evil ways that Satan is trying to teach to the world these days to make the world fall apart in horrid ways, but we all have help from God by our side, so we don't have much to worry about if we just stay in a good relationship with Him .

Think of this . With the way that the sky and pretty much the entire area all around us go dark in the evenings, we don't have to worry about fully losing all the light we need .

Just as in buildings, we too have light switches, and with those we have the opportunity to turn on the light that has been turned off by Satan . Doing that is a great way to make a good relationship with God . God is the one who is shining in that light, so when you get that light turned on, do a lot of praying to Him for His guidance and also for whatever you may need at that time .

Another way of saying this is like this . With all the people these days, some make the decision not to follow God and what He wants to teach everyone, but everyone is allowed to make their own personal choice, like are they going to follow God, or are they going to just be a person who is living by the secular ways that the world has to offer?

With Satan coming in and blocking the light for a lot of people, I guess we can say that God is the ROCK for these situations . With God being the Rock, that means that everyone will have a large amount of backup support from Him whenever they might need it .

He is the most stabilizing support that any person can get at any time and also from any location . Everyone needs support these days, but no one seems to realize that they can get the support that they need from God, but even if they don't acknowledge that God is our supporter, God will still help them out because He loves everyone .

It just takes some work on our side because we need to spread His Word to as many people as we are able to do because the more people we can help to become Christians, we can say that we have been turning on the light switches to the different rooms that each person is renting at this time .

Even though we might turn on the light switch, the light bulb might die . That would happen because Satan sells to almost all of us bad light bulbs, but it's hard to say when we are going to have any problems with them .

The main place to get the best light bulbs that will never give us any problems is from God . He just wants the best for everyone, and He loves everyone so much . To think of that should light up anybody's day more than what they were expecting .

If any of your neighbors aren't Christian, and they need help with new light bulbs, go over to their place and offer them some new ones made by God . That is another way of saying just go to them and spread the Word of God and tell them what He has done for you and other people you know in your lives .

Just remember to always fight the things that Satan tries to put into your life . God is on your side, so you will always win the fights against Satan if you just keep good communication with Him and do what He tells you to do .

Having God on your side through all those fights, either between you and another person or if you get involved in a fight with Satan, God is always there to support anyone who may need His help .

CHAPTER 2

God Is the Way, Even though He Was Slain

There are so many different options that a person has to choose from every day these days . But the most important one is if they are going to follow God, or if they are just going to be like the rest of the people who follow the ways Satan has come up with to pull us away from God .

Teaching your children about God and how good He is for them is something good to do because helping someone else to become a Christian and to following the teachings God has given us in the Bible is like helping them to win the largest amount that can be won with a lottery ticket .

God is not just the King who is ruling over everyone from heaven . There is also Jesus and the Holy Spirit . Jesus is the son of God, which means that they are a holy family, a very powerful one . The Holy Spirit is in that family too .

With having those three in that family, we have the choice whenever we need assistance as to which one we want to go to in prayer for that help, and if we don't know which one to choose, they will choose the proper one that will fully take care of that situation for us, which will make our lives a lot more relaxed .

Jesus was slain on a cross, back in the days when the people had to follow the religion that the Romans had been bringing into their country . Jesus arose from being dead after three days, and He helped so many people, and then He went to heaven .

We can say this to other people, "God is the way to go, try to make others know ." By doing this, it can help a lot of people to get to know God and the other two who are in His family, which is the best selection that anyone can get at any time these days .

Becoming a Christian and following God and His family will just turn out to be a rewarding time that is lived if you follow the rules He has laid out for everyone . They are easy rules to obey, so just try to keep away from all the things Satan might be doing to the world these days and just focus on God and His family up there in heaven .

Satan keeps trying to pull people away from God, but with the powerful work of God's love that works against everything that Satan is trying to do to everyone right now, we don't need to worry because God is more than able to defeat Satan at anything he is trying to do, but the final decision of it is made by a human because God has given us that as a gift . Because Jesus was hung on that cross back in the past,

God then gave all of us a lot of new choices they could make at any time they wanted to . The choices would either be helping them or others, or maybe just waiting until a new situation would arise, saying that people needed their help .

People have finally started to realize that the truth about God is the way in which they need to live their life . Also, a lot of them have started to feel a calling from God to go and spread the Word of God to whomever they might get into a conversation with at whatever time .

With the ways that Satan keeps trying to mess up everyone's lives, we don't really have that much to worry about if we keep a good relationship with God and the rest of His family (Jesus and the Holy Spirit) .

The reason why none of us have that much to worry about is because God is supremely more powerful than Satan is in any way, and with the countless number of followers God has, He will surely have the leadership over everything for all eternity in the most loving way .

Satan has his number of followers too, but with God being more powerful, there is no reason in most ways to worry about anything, so just follow God fully .

With all the people who have decided to follow Satan instead of God, the world has really become a true war land . That is because there is always a spiritual warfare going on between God and Satan at all times, and it's just up to us to make the final decision for which side we are going to follow .

CHAPTER 3

God Is the One, with Him We Have Fun

God is the leader and creator of everyone and everything here on earth with us right now; the problem is that there are so many people who just don't know the information about Him, and they keep trying hard to block it out of their lives .

That just means that those of us who are Christians, we need to get out into as many areas as we can and spread the Word of God to help other people realize that actually becoming a Christian is not a bad thing to do . It helps other people who aren't Christian, and with the information we bring to them, it really gives them a good chance at getting saved by God, but it just depends on what their final choice is going to be .

Getting into conversations with other people and maybe adding into it the information about God and how to become a member of His family is a great way to help people hopefully find their way to the road that will lead them to the best place that anyone wants to go to .

Building a relationship with God is like learning how to draw a picture . If a person is just hearing about God for the first time, and they want to find out more about God and His family, we can tell them that the best thing for them to do at that time is to go to church services on Sunday at whatever times the churches have them .

Keeping a relationship with God working strong in your life is fully a personal choice because it all depends on us if we follow the rules, and nothing turns out to be better than those results .

We just need to remember to follow along and walk the path that will lead us, and hopefully others, to the path into heaven .

The RULES that God has made for everyone to hopefully choose to follow are the Ten Commandments:

1. I am the Lord your God: You shall not have strange Gods before me .

2. You shall not take the name of the Lord your God in vain .

3. Remember to keep holy the Lord's Day .

4. Honor your father and your mother .

5. You shall not kill .

6. You shall not commit adultery .

7. You shall not steal .

8. You shall not bear false witness against you neighbor .

9. You shall not covet your neighbor's wife .

10. You shall not covet you neighbor's goods .

Those are really good rules to follow, but the only thing is that we need to inform people that the commandments are the best rules to follow these days because God made them .

Actually, depending on the way you do it, following through with the Ten Commandments can be something fun to do . Having fun by following the rules God has given us is the way to go .

In the same way that one of your neighbors might be telling other people in that area information about something, like a big sale coming up on a certain day, just start spreading the information about the Word of God in the way you have learned how to if you are feeling called to do that from God .

God calls on a lot of people to spread His Word, but He doesn't call on everyone . For those whom He does call on, they should go to a group like Youth With A Mission, which is a strong worldwide Christian group that trains people and goes to countless amounts of places to spread the Word of God to people in all the countries of the world .

There are other groups that people can get together with, and one of them is the Salvation Army, which is also a strong Christian group like YWAM . The Salvation Army has churches in numerous areas in a countless number of cities of the world to help people get to know God better than how they originally knew Him .

The best and main thing any person needs to do when they are going out to spread the Word of God is to start the day with a prayer to God requesting His help in that field of work . It seems like a large majority of people don't want to bother with the information that God has to offer, but He has many ways to attract them to it .

In total, helping other people get to know God and possibly become a Christian feels so rewarding when you know that you have helped someone else to accomplish that mark in their life .

CHAPTER 4

Spread the Word, Be Like a Bird

In cities where people live, both the Salvation Army and YWAM are doing things in the city, like walking down streets and talking to people, and they ask them questions and answer phone calls in their offices and answer any questions asked on the calls .

It's a great time when you get involved with either one of those groups because you learn how to get close with God and also how to help other people get close to Him in that same way, which is what everyone on this planet really needs to do . Building a good relationship with God is something that really helps a person's life because God created everything that is here right now, so that just truly makes Him everyone's King . When you are living somewhere and getting a call from

God to spread His Word, then start looking around the city for groups like YWAM or the Salvation Army .

Getting involved with either one of those groups will turn out to be a great way to spread the Word of God to as many people as you can reach in that surrounding area . Helping them in that way is truly the best way to help someone because it will last them for eternity if they decide to make the proper decision YWAM has camps and bases located in different areas all around the world right now where people can go and take training courses that teach them how to spread the Word of God to anybody they might be talking to at that certain time . The Salvation Army is placed all over the world in different cities in many different countries . They are spreading the Word of God, and they also have stores open to help people

who need different things, which they sell at a low price .

The Salvation Army reaches out to a countless amount of people every day, spreading the Word of God in a very solidified way . That means that they are a group that, in a way, fights for God in everything that they do . They also try hard to get as many other people as possible to join their army, which fights against Satan at all times, just like the other Christians do .

Figuring out all the details is something that we need to do to be aware, and we need to inform everyone about how Satan is getting into everyone's lives and how he is working so hard to mess up everybody's entire lives . Things like this can be confusing to understand, but with help from God, we are able to get through times that Satan is trying to mess up for all of us .

With the world being separated into families and groups and also, of course, the larger-size groups known as countries, that just makes it easier for Satan to get his hands in there and to try to rule over everyone who chooses not to walk the pathway God has made for everyone to follow .

The more people we spread the Word of God to and also help by answering any questions that they might have about that, they will hopefully start going to church services on Sundays and changing their life in a way that will bring them closer to God .

Everyone thinks of God and Satan in their own ways .

Those ways are like these:

GOD – The creator and loving father and king of the entire world .

SATAN – The evil leader of the people who do not decide to become a Christian .

Tell as many other people as you want to about God and the details about what He does for people every day . God is just the most loving god that can be found anywhere, and He is always a reliable one to use for anything you might need—just make sure you pray for others first .

CHAPTER 5

Working with God: A Solid Rod

No matter what kind of a life that a person may have been living, God is always there next to them to help them out in any way they might need help of any kind at that certain time.

Having God by your side through any circumstance can make your connection with God much stronger and more stable, so that means that there is less fear . All you need to do is remember to follow God .

Just think of God as this kind of a rod: He is a fishing rod, and we are the fishermen and women who are fishing with God also as the bait to get as many of the other people to acknowledge that they need to become Christian .

A rod is also something that is very strong and stable to have by your side that you grip with your hands to solidify your walk with God and also your mission to spread His Word to as many people as you can possibly reach .

If we all just studied the Bible for more information God has taught us through all those years, we would all be a lot smarter and closer to God . Being closer to God is something that everyone should aim in their life these days because living a life close to God makes the road much easier to travel on .

And also, another form of a rod that people might think God is like is a cane made for people who are either blind or have a medical disability that makes it very hard for them to walk on their own . With God being that cane, anybody who wants to use that cane just needs to accept Him as their Savior and follow His teachings, and by mainly using the cane (God), they will get led to a calmer and more peaceful way to hopefully live their life .

This will probably be a bit confusing at first, but there is a way to stop that confusion . At a time when you might get a feeling to use the cane, just switch it in a gentle way in your mind . Try to picture how God is so loving and helpful and how He is always next to us, ready for any situation that might arise .

For those of us who don't need to use canes and also never use fishing rods, we should keep our ears open when we are out because we might get into a conversation with someone who either does not know about God, or just has decided to fully live their life in the worldly way that Satan has created .

When you get into a conversation with someone, try to bring into the conversation about how good God is, or you can ask questions based on their religious faith . If questions start to arise from them, just answer them the best way that you are able to at that time . Usually answering questions that come from people who are starting to get attracted to God and the full religion of Christianity helps them to find their way, like which church they should attend, and also, depending on what their lifestyle is like at that time, if they are going to need to change that in any way .

We all just need to continue to work with God as much as we possibly can every day . With the work schedules people get from their jobs and school that might cut down the amount of time that we are able to work with God, we should still setout time for Him .

When you're working with God, you're being stabilized with a rod (God), and you can take that rod with you anywhere you want to go and include it in anything that you might be doing at that time .

In the end, just take God by His hands and learn as much as you can about Him by going to church or maybe even just constantly praying to Him and letting Him lead you through your life fully .

CHAPTER 6

Be Fond to Build a Bond

There is a countless number of things these days that people are fond about, but all of them need to realize that God is the one they should be the fondest of . Having God at the top of your list is the best way to make any kind of a list .

God is the one who works with us to stabilize our relationship with Him, which I guess we can call a bond . Having a bond with God is very expensive, worth much more than the ones you find at the banks . Just remember that God has nothing to do with money unless you ask Him for help in your finances .

God helps in all situations that any person might be going through in their life these days if that person just goes into prayer and requests help from God after asking to be forgiven for their sins .

For those of us who are Christians, we should try telling other people about the grace of God and how loving He is and how He truly proves every day that He is still here next to us, so we have a solid bond with Him every day of our lives if we decide to go to church and possibly become a Christian .

Something that everybody is told to do these days is to do things that help out the other people living in your community, like your neighbors and friends . It doesn't matter if you are doing something to help them all out already, but you can also try hard to spread the total information about God to everyone who is living in your neighborhood if you are able to do that .

Going out through your neighborhood gives you a really good opportunity to tell anyone you might meet all the information about God, which will hopefully lead them to attend a couple of church services that will lead them to make their choice of maybe becoming a full Christian .

When anyone is spreading the Word of God to other people, they need to be aware that Satan might be sticking his hands into that area to start a fight between our side and his side . We need to remember that we have God on our side, so we will win that fight because God is superior to Satan .

Being bonded with all three of them—God, Jesus, and the Holy Spirit—is actually the best bond that anyone can get anywhere . It is like that because of the way they are bonded together and work together through everything . It doesn't matter though because with the way that Satan keeps getting into everyone's lives, they are always by our side, ready to help us through the war we are fighting against Satan .

There are also so many reasons why people can't bond with God and the other two, and here is one of those reasons . This is the main reason, and it is we need to keep control of our sins, and also whenever we might sin, we need to pray for forgiveness .

Those people who can't bond with God for reasons like that one still have the opportunity to bond with Him if they attend any church services and hear all the truth about Him . Usually after people have attended church services a few times, they feel called to become a Christian, which is one of the best choices any person can make for themselves .

Actually, it isn't just one of the best choices, but it is the absolute best choice out of any that anyone can make these days . Just keep in your mind what kind of friends you will be making and what family you will be joining and what more relaxed options you will have to make compared to living a secular life .

If we all just focus more on living a life completely aimed at God and also following His teachings fully, there would definitely be more of a chance of the world building a bond with Him . That is the way to go . It's like living in a house He has built for you and everyone else .

CHAPTER 7

Satan's Not the Way, Listen to What God Says

So many people these days follow Satan/Lucifer, and they are a religion called Satanists . In that religion, they are completely fighting against God and everything that has to do with Christianity .

Some people join up with Satan's religion because they are thinking it's the cool thing to do at that time, and their minds can't be changed to follow God, Who is the leader of love .

But it's not all their minds that can't be changed because making the choice between religions is fully a personal choice . Getting into a group, if any, there might be a few Satanists there, so we need to try to spread the Word to them through whatever details you think would be beneficial at that time because there is no telling if they might change their mind and start following God, which is, of course, the proper way to go . Maybe if one of your children has decided to become a Satanist, try to get them to go to a few church services with you so they will be hit with the information and the love from God, which would have a very good effect on the battle between God and Satan, which is not just happening out in the spiritual world, but is happening in us as well .

Adults also make decisions, like if they are going to be a Christian or follow Satan . A lot of adults are smart, and they make the decision to follow God, but the rest just follow the world, which is Satan . Following Satan can be painful and also a very deadly thing to do, but if they notice those things and then change their minds and want to follow God instead, all they need to do is pray to Him and ask for His help .

God and Satan/Lucifer have always been at war with each other, and one of the ways to help God win that war is to follow His teachings and to block Satan as much as we can from coming into our lives and trying to disturb our walk with God .

Even though there might be a time when you think that Satan has been completely defeated, there is a good chance that you might find out that Satan is still doing as much evil things all around the world as he can do at one time . The only real thing that we can do about that is to pray hard against that to get as much of God's help because this will be a definite time that we all will be needing His help .

Making yourself a Christian is something that was given to everyone, like a gift . And when you are a Christian, if you are following the basic guidelines for this religion, you will find that more places accept you and the things you are offering more than before .

God has a very big "House," which is open to hold any amount of people who want to join His family . Whoever joins His family will automatically be accepted into His "House," and the leader of that household, of course, is God, so with us being His good children, we need to follow His ways and maybe see if we can get that particular information about Him spread to others .

Going on a date with someone never sounds bad, but just try to think of a relationship with God like this—you are always out on a date with Him . He is fully there for you or anyone else, and is also ready to help in any way too .

Fighting also happens in majority of families, but if you keep up-to-date at church with their lessons at their services on Sundays, there is a high chance you will learn a way to keep those forms of fighting out of your life .

We never have to worry about fighting with God, and the reason for that is because He is just fully purehearted, and it's almost like He's made of gold, but you never know, He might have made Himself fully out of gold .

We all need to have that good bond with God to really live a stable life, but there is one thing that we need to try to do . We need to try to inform others about how living with a stable life that God has given you is one of the best choices to make . We must also tell them the outline of how God is superior to Satan in every way possible .

CHAPTER 8

For Truth and Love, Follow God, the Dove

All three of them—God, Jesus, and the Holy Spirit—are completely full of everlasting love for everyone here on earth right now, even though none of us are fully worthy of that love until we start following them with our minds wide open at all times .

They also teach us, all throughout the Bible, the proper ways in which we should be truthful and loving in our lifestyles . When we go to church services on Sundays, we might learn some of that information there also .

It is hard these days to fully understand the differences between all the different religions, but when a person is trying to make their decision of which one they are going to be following, God will strongly lead them toward being a Christian .

When friends get together, it's always better for them when they are being fully truthful with each other in their conversations and everything else that they do together .

Families always keep getting together like friends do and have fun and do other things as well . Examples of when family and friends get together are these:

1 . Weddings, which are times when love is truly shown, and sometimes people also become Christians when they get married

2 . Funerals, where people are mainly crying over the loss of

either a friend or family . Lots of prayer is done during that time because every person wants to make sure that the person who died goes to heaven once they have died .

Some families, whether they are believers in any religion or not, have real lives to live . But with other families, things just seem to go wrong in the world these days that it all keeps messing up their lives . For help with that, they need to know that if they keep going to God in prayer, He would definitely be helping them through all that with His full, loving, and caring heart .

Getting into a good solid relationship with God, Jesus, and the Holy Spirit is a very important topic for any person's life these days . The reason why it is so important is that when a person actually builds that relationship, they will feel so much more stable than normal .

A lot of people think that when they first become a Christian, they are going to be making a relationship with only Jesus . The truth of that situation though is that the person who does that will be making that relationship with all three of them . The reason why it may be confusing is that the three of them are one (God), but they also work on their own at times .

If a person is having a hard time building a relationship with another person, say, for a friendship or maybe dating, which can lead into a marriage relationship, they can go to God for help in these situations for any reason that may arise in their life at that time .

KEEP IN GOD COMMUNICATION WITH GOD EACH DAY OF YOUR LIFE

CHAPTER 1

God Grows Us like A Garden, Satan Gets on Us like Bees

God has created all of mankind ever since He created the entire world . Working with God is something that we all need to make ourselves focus on because when we concentrate on having a good time with God every day of our lives, it will probably pay us back in a very profitable way, which is spiritual .

When the men and women back in those early ages started to mess up the ways in which they were living, Satan started to get into their lives and also into everything else . But a fair amount of other people who were staying faithful to God prayed to Him and asked Him to protect them from what Satan was doing at that time because they didn't want to leave the loving ways God was giving all of them .

A lot of different situations came up for all those people back in those times because there were different royalties who were ruling over different areas, and they all seemed like they had different gods that they were worshipping . There were wars between the leaders until one of them fully led their group to take over the others and have a bigger land portion to live on than before . What happened then is similar to what is happening these days .

Keeping in prayer with God every day is a good way to stay in good communication with Him whenever you need to talk to Him . One way to picture praying to Him is like being on a phone call with God, and we can talk with Him as long as we want any day of any year of our life .

Being in good communication with God as much as we can possibly be is something that we should definitely try hard to acquire because we will actually learn more than what we ever thought we would have been able to learn .

Lives can go on a lot longer than what a lot of people are thinking these days, considering even the medical problems and the murders happening everywhere . There are some people living into their hundreds, but that is rare . Still, it is a blessing from God .

All of us are always fighting against Satan, but a lot of us might not notice that yet or believe that is true . If everyone just took some time to go to a church service and see if any of the information from that taught them anything, they might change their outlook on Satan and God .

There is also the big spiritual warfare going on between God and Satan all day long every day of the year, and that is something that majority of us cannot get ourselves away from . If we all decide to follow God, we just need to keep ourselves focused on Him, and in any way that we can, we need to defy Satan from getting into our lives . That battle can be won if we just remember to stay in constant prayer with God about that topic and the way or ways it is affecting us .

Showing God's love to others is a proven way to bring other people to become believers in God and everything He is offering to all of us . Showing that part of God is also a way of making people feel more secure in their walk with God, so help those other people out and try to do it .

CHAPTER 2

What Does God Do in People's Lives?

There is a countless amount of people living all around the world right now, and it is really hard to say what God is doing in each person's life because He works with each person separately and also in such a loving way .

All times can be either easy to get by or rather confusing, but it's hard to say which way it's going to be when we are working with God . To let the process go through a bit more smoothly than what we were expecting, we need to stay close to God and be fully open to His ideas and His ways so we can work together in a nice and easy way .

People are being healed by God all around the world each day of every year, and the only problem with that is that sometimes, some people don't get convinced that God is actually here with us wherever we go and helping us out in whatever ways we might be needing at those times .

The main reason why some people don't become convinced is because Satan still manages to stick his hands into those situations and mess things up for those people, just out of the way he hates everything that was created by God .

GOD IS THE MAN TAKE HIS HANDS

CHAPTER 1

Spread the Word

There is a great group to get with these days if you are feeling called to spread the Word of God to as many other people around the world as you are able to . That group is called Youth With A Mission (YWAM) . Their head base is in Kona, Hawaii, and they have hundreds of other bases located all around the world .

First, with YWAM, a person takes a three-month course where they learn how to spread the Word of God, and then they go on a three-month outreach to a different country to practice spreading the Word .

When I was with YWAM, I took my training in Melbourne, Australia, back in 2000, and then I did my outreach at the Olympics in Sydney, Australia, and also other places located all around Australia .

My parents also got involved with YWAM back when I was a child . They took their training at the head base in Kona, Hawaii . After their three months of training, the group went to Singapore, Malaysia, and also a lot of different places in Thailand, like Bangkok, which is completely overpopulated . While we were there, we never missed out on the opportunity

T H E F A M I L Y L I V I N G I N W A R M T H

of telling others about God and hopefully leading them to join His family .

There is another good group to get with that people can use

just for church on Sundays and also for clothing and food . It is called the Salvation Army .

The Salvation Army helps out people in the city who may not have enough money for food or clothing or for an apartment . People in the cities make donations to them all the time . The donations that are made help so many people . It is just great to know the amount of people who a person might help .

The Salvation Army has stores in cities that are good for people who are low in income . Their stores sell clothing, furniture, food, dishes, and a lot of other things people might have given to them to be sold in the store .

So many people these days are Christian, and a lot of people are either going by another religion or just not believing in anything . Christianity is the most popular religion, which is out all around the world these days, good for anyone to use . It is also the perfect one that will take a person to heaven when they die if they follow the rules that God has laid out for everyone to follow .

Helping other people to build a relationship with God in their life is something good to do because having a strong relationship with God is the best one that you can get anywhere . Majority of people these days need to be prayed for because of either medical or financial problems or other reasons . It doesn't matter what the reasons might be, but God

will always help in His own calendar .

You don't always have to buy something to help someone or donate money to help . You can pray for anyone, even the entire world . By taking God by His hands, we can walk with Him anywhere we want to go to .

But it is still good to do those things if you are able to them . Everybody has to watch how they spend their income these days because everything is expensive . Everybody feels like they are poor at times, and there is a rather large size of people who are poor (you know, without money and food) . They need help from the people who do bring in an income from a job .

God helps so many people every day of each year . He helps everyone with medical problems, financial problems, or any other kind of problems we might have at that time .

God is like a doctor for our lives . Whenever we are having problems, we can go to God and pray for Him to heal us or to show us what to do in those situations . He is the most loving and caring father that can be found anywhere around the world .

Spreading the information about Him to everyone else is something that needs to be done these days . There are so many different techniques that people can use to spread the Word of God . They can do that in pretty much any place they want to, all around the world . Helping other people to get to know God as their Savior is something great to do because it just feels so relaxing, and it is also fun .

The main reason why it's good to help other people get to know God is because God will help anyone who is a part of His family . He will never stop showing His love for members because He loves everyone . The only thing is when people are sinning and doing bad things all the time, that is when He turns His head away from them .

A lot of people these days have chosen to follow other religions, but the majority are still following Christianity . There are still so many people all around the world who have not heard of being a Christian, so what we need to do is to spread the info about it when we go out each day and pray hard that the people that we have informed will hopefully become Christians .

The main reason why it is good to spread the Word of God to as many other people as you can is because God is as important as money and food for everyone to survive . It may be hard work to get them to understand the details, but it is fully worth doing .

A lot of people get confused with the information about Christianity, but it's easy to understand why they get confused about the details of all the different religions . The majority of the different religions started in other countries many years ago .

But still, with spreading the Word of God to other people in all those different countries, it just helps out those people in such a great way by teaching them how to walk with God and to have Him as a part of their lives .

All in all, spreading the Word of God is one of the best things that a Christian can do at any time of the year . A person can start spreading the Word to others to whoever they might get into a conversation with .

We can talk to people in cafés and bus stops or any other locations in the cities or towns, and we can tell the information of God to them in our conversations that we might hopefully get into .

Just remember that it is not just fun to spread the Word of God, but when you do it, your relationship with God will become stronger and also more empowered . Building a strong relationship with God is the most important thing for anyone to do .

CHAPTER 2

Show the Love of God

Everybody always says how they love to help out as many other people as they can each day, but that is a lie . A lot of people are either too poor or scared to help out those other people, but they may still find certain ways to donate money when they are able to afford it .

God is giving all of us His love every day of each year . He also teaches us all how to show His love in the same way He shows it to us . That may sound difficult, but it can actually be rather easy to do .

Everyone who is alive needs to know about God . God's information also fills a person up with so much love and relaxation . They can use that information in any way they want to . Doctors use that info when they are in surgery and when they are doing similar procedures for God to lead them in those things .

The way that the doctors use the information about God in the surgeries and other things is that a lot of them pray before they go into surgery, asking God to guide them and help them through the entire procedure they are about to do at those times . God 90 percent of the time answers prayers, but not always right after it was prayed . Often, we have to wait for a bit for our prayers to be answered . One thing that we can be sure of is that God loves everyone, and He is always here, right next to everyone's side to help them through their life .

Helping anyone else for any reason, regardless of age, is a

good reason for showing love and care and also giving help to whoever you might be able to do that for at this current time . So many people just refuse to build a relationship with God, so their lives are just so full of sin that they are going to go to hell when they die unless they build a relationship with

God, but so many people just refuse to do that .

Those people just need to realize that building one of those relationships with God is one of the absolute best things that you can do these days . going to church and learning more about God and what to do with His information and how to show His love to everyone else that you might come into contact with is a really good thing to learn all together .

We, as believers in God, need to help those other people realize that when any of us build a relationship with Him, it makes our lives more solidly stable in their outcomes .

We are all encouraged to spread the Word of God, do what God tells us to do when we pray to Him (because a lot of the time He leads us all in His own timing), go out and either help people by telling them about God, or just show them the love of God by helping them financially or similar ways like that .

Showing the love of God to everyone, even to yourself, is something really good to do . It doesn't just help you build good relationships with others and also God, but when you are doing that, it is so relaxing and peaceful to go through with .

You can show other people the love of God by making donations by way of either money or food or clothing or thing like furniture to the Salvation Army or other associations like that one to help out anyone who needs some help .

The Christmas season is one of the best times each year that the Salvation Army uses the kettles for fundraising to raise money for the needy . Everyone just feels like they can give amounts of their pocket change when they see the kettles on the corners of the streets and inside some of the malls and stores when it is raining .

Love from God can come as quickly as a coffee pod . It can also be so strong and full of warmth, teaching us all the aspects about life that we need to know at that current time .

God also blesses us in whatever way He sees fit . The main reasons why He does that is because He is our father, a great loving one who cares for everyone and all things He has created .

People say that love can be shown with flowers or gifts or by doing art for someone, but the true actual way to receive love is to go to God for it . All you have to do is pray and request it in your prayers .

When you receive love from God, just thank Him for it in your prayers, and then continue to pray for whatever else you may need to pray for at that current time . He is always here by our sides to assist us in whatever way we need help at that current time, so if we just pray to Him and ask for assistance in those areas of our lives, He will come in and help us out .

Love and care have always been the most important feelings to show toward other people . The reason why it has been so important is because those two feelings just seem to be the main two feelings God has .

Everybody shows love to their family and friends, but there is a very small portion of us who do not show love to anyone or anything out there at this current time . Everyone just needs to realize how important love is for everybody's lives .

We have people in our world who are sick with different kind of illnesses and also people who may have been born with some form of a dysfunction to either their body or their minds . We should really pray for those people every day, if we can remember to do that, because God always backs us up behind every prayer we make .

God always comes through and helps us all the way through our lives if we actually believe in Him and maybe even share the information about Him to others . That just makes our lives easier to live, most of the time, but a person just has to remember to continue to build that relationship with God as much as they possibly can .

God is such a loving father to everyone who is here on earth right now, and the ones in space too . When He answers our prayers, He chooses all sorts of different ways to do that, like what form of timing and also to which actual person it is going to affect the most if everyone just follows His lead .

If everyone just got smarter and decided to follow God in their walk of life, everybody's lives would just be so much more under control and peaceful . That is the form of a lifestyle that pretty much everyone wants to get, but they just need to realize that they all have to work to accomplish that feature .

Showing God's love to as many other people as you can and also maybe helping any of those other people out if they need any kind of help at that time is something good to do... so do it .

CHAPTER 3

Go to All the Lands and Tell of the Man

Any person these days can go on a trip with family or friends or just by themselves, and on that trip, they might spread the Word of God . It's hard to say where any person is going to go on a trip before they start planning it, but that's because there are so many places in the world to choose from . We can go to pretty much all the lands in Africa, all the states in America, all the provinces in Canada, almost the entire region of South America, Russia, Japan, Australia...and so many others . It's just great to have a selection like that open to us, but the only problem is that it can get so darn expensive

for a trip to somewhere else .

All other people in all those other countries need to be informed about God because in a lot of those countries, they practice other religions that seem to be running everybody's lives .

All the people in our cities need to know as well, so talking about God and the details about Christianity in conversations we might get into each day is something good to do . It informs other people about God and also gives them the option to make the proper choice or not .

There are also numerous Christian groups all around the world that people can get associated with to learn how to spread the Word of God to other people in the cities where they may be living or wherever they may go to spread His information to everyone else who is out there right now .

The Salvation Army is pretty much in all areas of the cities worldwide . They spread the Word, and they also help people by assisting them to get clothing and furniture . They also have churches open on Sundays .

The Salvation Army also has things like camps in areas, and at their churches, they have little summer lessons for things like singing and playing different musical instruments, which is something that a lot of people have to do these days for financial reasons .

Another Christian group we can all get together with is called Youth With A Mission (YWAM) . This group is located everywhere worldwide . They have bases where a person can have training in for three months, and then go on outreach for three months to possibly another country or maybe on the other side of the same country that they are in .

All in all, spreading the Word of God to as many others as you are able to spread the Word to in a day is something good to do . It is so good because just think of how much God loves everyone and how much He helps us all . He even loves the ones who are completely against Him for some reason .

When we spread the information about God, we can also use that as an opportunity to build friendships or other types of relationships with other people who we might know . Helping anybody else to get to know God as their true leader is a fulfilling thing to do in anybody's life . We all just need to remember the basic rules we have to follow for being a Christian .

Praying a lot and also reading parts of the Bible God might be leading you to read from are all good things to do because in those situations, God will aid the person who is doing that form of material work . Volunteering some of your time every so often to places and people who are needing the aid of other people like us (who are able to give them financial aid or help them in person) is a commendable thing to do as well .

Going to Bible studies in your churches is something good to do because it helps everyone learn so much more out of the Bible and also a lot more about God . Learning about those two things, which are the two of the most important things to learn about these days, is good to do for anyone's life . God is an artist, and we are the pieces of art that He makes all the time to make the display of art in the "museum" (the world) stand out, displaying all the different aspects that He may have created to stand out in all of us if we decide to

choose Him as our Savior .

He is our loving father, Savior, and God, and with Him giving us that much love at times, it is just great to combine with Him and to strengthen our walk we have with Him at these current times .

We all do have the problems of Satan getting into our lives and messing them up with all his anger and hate and all the different forms of evil . What we need to do to find our ways around those things is to pray to God and request help in that certain area of our lives .

Satan can make people sick in many different ways, and that can also include mental illnesses and broken bones . The good thing is that if that ever happens to you, just pray to God, and there is a high chance that He will answer those prayers right away .

God loves all of mankind . With the way that He has blessed all of us with His love, we should be so thankful for that rich gift He has blessed us all with . One thing we do need to do is to inform other people who may not know about the information of Christianity . By doing that, it will help everyone to become orientated with Christianity in a more secure way .

There are millions of people who are living around the world these days who are Christians, maybe even more than that amount . We need to remember that God loves everyone, and anyone who accepts Him as their Leader will be guided into heaven when they die .

Going out into the neighborhoods and getting into conversations with people who we may not know is something good to do because it is an easy way to spread the Word of God .

CHAPTER 4

God Is the King, Jesus Is His Son

With God creating everything that is in the universe we are living in, we should know that our Lord God is so thoughtful and careful towards everything . When we need help from Him, all we need to do is pray to Him and ask for the type of help we need at that current time .

Some people think that God only helps out rich men and women, so something that we really need to do is to spread the information about how God actually helps all of mankind every day of the year .

With God and Jesus being our royalty family, we need to praise and treat them like the most important ones in our lives, which we know that they are at all times in our lives .

The Holy Spirit is also a part of that family . By getting into communication with all three of them in prayer when we need to really helps a lot . The Holy Spirit, when we pray, comes and helps us out a lot of the time, but sometimes the Spirit is too busy already .

We are blessed by the love and care God, Jesus, and the Holy Spirit show everyone every day . The only thing to add to that is that the people who want to become closer to God's family just need to pray to God and ask Him to lead them through their entire lives . It is the best family relationship that can ever be made on this planet, so everyone really needs to make a personal relationship with the Lord for the rest of their lives .

God is our strong, caring, and loving King who is ruling over the entire world . A lot of people may not know about that, so they really need to be informed, which would give them a very good chance at becoming a Christian and going to heaven when they die .

Becoming a Christian is something very important to do in everyone's life . It's important because there are so many good Christian friends that can be made all around the world, and there are also a lot of people who believe in other religions or have no belief at all . We can help those people by telling them the full-truth information about Christianity, which might bring them toward becoming a fully dedicated Christian believer .

There are also lots of problems with the world these days, like with large amounts of people being racist against other countries . But all men and women from all countries around the world are equal and loved by God . I find it pathetic the way that those people treat those other people . They just need to realize that everybody is equal to each other .

Nobody really knows how to handle those problems, but if everyone just got to know more information about the Lord and what He has planned for everybody, the world would be a much calmer and safer place to live in .

God comes to anyone who prays to Him for help as quick as an ambulance gets to areas to help when there is an emergency . God is the best helper that anyone can find anywhere . That info needs to be spread around the world so everyone will start to have a stronger relationship with the Father .

Having a strong relationship with God, Jesus, and the Holy Spirit is one of the most absolute precious things any person can do for themselves these days . It guarantees them a much calmer and more peaceful life to live and also a ride into heaven when we die, which is the true place of peace .

When you actually think about it, we rely on God for help with about everything in our lives . That goes down into much deeper detail than that, like the secrets of what we have to do at work, which might become illegal .

God helps everybody out for whatever reason they may need to pray about at that current time . He may not help right away, like it could take a period of time until we find out when He got it timed in for . He always helps out though, and it is just up to us to remember to keep a solid relationship with the Father to build a strong lifeline in all the families around the world .

Going to church on Sundays is a time each week when God, Jesus, and the Holy Spirit teach us lots of different things they may want us to do with our lives . When God plans something for someone's life, we can be sure that those plans are mainly going to carry through peacefully and also in an entertaining way that will help us to live through our lives .

Some people don't realize this, but if you have a child, take them to church on Sunday morning and see how they react to the lessons in Sunday school . Educating our children these days in that way is something really important to do because it improves their knowledge about God, and getting started at a young age is good to do because then it can help out more people than just you .

The lessons the pastors preach to all of us on Sundays come from communication with God, Jesus, and the Holy Spirit . When we are at the churches to learn those lessons, we need to remember to keep those working in our lives . Being a Christian is a true way to build a solid relationship with a very large amount of other people and also to build that same kind of relationship with God, Jesus, and the Holy Spirit .

Having a solid relationship with any person or definitely with God, Jesus, and the Holy Spirit is one of the best things that any person can plan out for themselves . They just need to keep doing what is needed to actually maintain those relationships because the ones with other people will help them through their lives, and the other ones will help through eternity .

God is not just the King, but He is the Holy King who has been ruling over the world since He created it . With God being the Holy King, that gives us so many more options to choose from in our lives to make our lives the living way that He sort of planned out for us .

Having such a large number of options to choose from throughout our lives can make our lives much more relaxing . One thing that we should be remembering to do is to thank God for giving us all those options and also helping us in any other way, which He may have helped us at that current time .

CHAPTER 5

The Stressful Times We Go through with Satan

We all wake up in the morning and start working with God, but after that, Satan comes by and tries to get deep into our lives and mess them up . The ways that Satan can mess up our lives can be in pretty much any way, so when we start to notice it happening in our life, we need to start praying to the Lord for His help so we can fully get through those stressful times .

The lessons that we learn from God definitely help out with our battle against Satan and also all those many evil ways of living we are trying to keep ourselves away from . There are so many different ways these days where Satan is trying to mess up our lives and also our relationships with our Father God . If we just stay aware and keep praying about it, our relationships should be kept good, so we shouldn't have much to worry about .

Most of those stressful, confusing, and painful times that we can go through with Satan are mainly done spiritually in our lives . With them being done in that way, we don't really

THE FAMILY LIVING IN WARMTH

have much to worry about because God comes in quickly and strongly to get us through those periods .

With so many people around the entire world worshipping Satan these days, we really need to get the information out to everyone about how God is superior to Satan . We also need to share the peaceful ways He uses to help us get through any of those stressful times .

Another thing we should really be focusing on these days is helping as many other people as we can to get them to understand the love God is handing out to everybody on earth every day . That can tend to be rather confusing, but God leads us and helps us through everything if we just pray to Him and ask Him to teach us the way that we should be doing His things in our lives at this current time .

It actually may not just be people who are Christians who get affected by Satan in all those different ways, but really, it is everyone who is here on earth who can get affected by Satan . The problems with that are that so many of those people are worshippers of all sorts of different religions, and we really need to tell them the info about God and the way that He helps against Satan every day of each year of our lives .

Working with God every day is a good way to start a holy business function, like having a personal relationship with Him for our entire life . Having a good bond with God throughout our lives is absolutely the best thing that anyone can do for themselves at any time during these current times . It can be like a business function with God because it's similar to the places where we all are working out of these days and building friendships and also possible careers that will bring us in enough money to pay our bills and to get us what we need at that current time .

Finding other Christians at work to make friendships with is something that all people can do with whoever they

D AN H O F F MAN

might be working with at this current time . We are allowed to make friends with anyone we want to, but doing that with other Christians only is the actual best way that we can choose in that topic .

The reason why it is the best way for that topic is because with you and your friends being Christians, all of you can bond together easier and also have that nice solid bond with God, Jesus, and the Holy Spirit . After you have learned how to make that bond with everyone, including the three in heaven, that is definitely information that you should share with anyone who you might be able to .

When our pastors preach to all of us on Sundays, we can really learn so much more from their sermons, and those also help us to bond in a much stronger way with God and everyone in His family . With being able to do that, we should really take advantage of it as much as we possibly can .

Doing volunteer work around our communities is really something great that God would like us all to be doing each day . We don't have to go into businesses, but we can just help others who meet in stores or on the streets in ways they may need help at that time .

There are many different businesses these days that are out there for all of us to volunteer with . The names of those are the Salvation Army, Youth With A Mission, and many more . Majority of these groups are Christians .

There are so many different topics and options for all the current things we have to do in our lives . But at times, the government helps us through those things a bit, but God definitely helps us all out much better than the government or anyone else is able to .

If we just remember to solidly use God's help when we need it and also spread around that information about Him, we can be sure of a calmer and more peaceful life . Having a life like that is truly a pure gift from God . Gifts come down from God all the time, and when He blesses us with any of those gifts, we should be fully thankful and maybe even worship Him for a while to let Him know how thankful we truly are .

So when we are using God's help and also sharing that help in the forms of volunteer work, telling information, and many more, we are also sharing a portion of God's help to everyone else in a helpful way .

All in all, living a life with God leading it is the absolute best way that anyone can really live their life . God, Jesus, and the Holy Spirit give so much stableness in a person's lifestyle that they can make anyone's lifestyle so much better for everyone to live every day .

CHAPTER 6

There Is Always a Spiritual Battle Happening

In every person's life, we all tend to go through different battles, fights, and wars, but still there is that one battle that's the same for everybody—the spiritual battle . God definitely helps us with the spiritual battles that we can go through at any time in our lives .

The things that we learn from those battles really tend to help us all out because our teacher is God . Our Lord always defeats Satan and his evil ways, so when we are fighting a spiritual battle between God, Satan, and us, with us being fully on God's side we should have nothing really to worry about but just to rely on God defeating Satan in that matter .

Even people who are committed Christians tend to get into deep and intense spiritual battles throughout their lives . We need to introduce the belief of Christianity to all those other people who are living everywhere else all around the world these days . By doing that, the world will become more like a golden planet for everyone to live in .

The spiritual battles, the fights, and the wars also have the Holy Spirit on our side mainly, the same way with Jesus and God, but every time, they have Satan in them, who is always fighting against us . With God and the other two of them being on our side at all times, we don't really have that much to worry about because they redeem us from our sins, and we can build good and strong relationships with all three of them at all times throughout our lives .

At times these days, some people who are not Christian- faith believers still tend to really get into spiritual battles . It seems, though, like the ones that they get into are mainly because their lives are filled with the ways that Satan is saying to live their lives, and they just tend to obey that, not thinking first about which way that might lead them .

If everybody really wants a peaceful and calmer life, then what they all really need to learn to do is how to follow God and His ways of living, which He has made for all of us to follow because that will bring us to more peace and also make us much calmer throughout our lives .

All people are different in so many different ways these days that it can make it difficult to make any kind of a relationship with anyone these days . That doesn't just mean people who you might be trying to make friends with or to date . At times, it is even difficult with God . The times that we run into that difficultness is when Satan comes up and tries to block the doorway between us and Him so we cannot get into a good and solid contact with our Lord .

For all people, throughout their lives, if they are Christians or not, they can have difficulties with their personal relationship with God, Jesus, and the Holy Spirit . All our pastors at our churches are giving really good sermons on Sundays that teach us at times a bit of a lesson on how to defeat Satan fully in those spiritual battles .

So yes, there are those other times throughout each week to do things, but the main thing that we should really get memorized and into our lives is going to church every Sunday, either in the morning or in the evening .

Going to church services is not only a great time to bond with other people, but the main reason why any person should go to church is to make a secure relationship with God and also to learn all the information about Him in deep detail .

At the church services, we will also be singing and praising God and sometimes getting into a time of deep worship . Worshipping the Lord is one of the absolute best things that anyone can do for their relationship with the Father, Jesus, and the Holy Spirit .

So if every person these days knew the information about God, Jesus, and the Holy Spirit and decides to accept them into their lives, there is a very high chance that would make the world a much more peaceful place for everybody to live in these days .

A spiritual battle or fight or war can sort of be thought of like a fight in a boxing ring . With the way that Satan can hold us down when he starts those fights in our lives, we start praying, and by praying, God gives us holy boxing gloves to use to battle against Satan and his ways .

The only real times when nobody seems to go through those battles and fights is when we are all in our childhood years . In those times, we are just too innocent to really understand the full detail about the topic .

A main problem with battles, wars, and fights these days is that every day, all around the world, there are millions of those types of fights being fought between people . People these days just don't recognize that those spiritual battles really need to be fought against as soon as they start to occur in our lives . All we need to do is as soon as we start to notice them in our life, we need to pray to God and ask for His help in the matter .

After God has helped us to defeat a spiritual battle or war or fight, our lives will be easier to live until Satan gets his hands in there again and messes up our spiritual walk with God . But the usual timing of those fights is rare, so we should live easy .

CHAPTER 7

Bonding with as Many Others as Possible

God teaches us throughout the Bible and in the church services that we really need to bond with as many other people as we possibly can at that this current time . He doesn't just teach us in those two things, but when He finds a proper opening in our lives, He comes in and gives us all sorts of lessons and suggestions throughout our lives .

There are so many ways to bond with other people that it can take quite a while to actually make a good relationship with someone else . Everybody wants to have a friendship with someone who is just like they are, and the best way to find friends like that is to look for other people to be your friends who are also Christians .

To get through the time frames in our days, a lot of prayers are usually needed in every person's life every day of every year . Any prayers that we make and send to God always get fully responded to, but we may not know when He is going to respond to our prayers .

We can bond and make friendships at the places where we work and go to school and when we're walking down the streets as well . And with the chances to do that at those places, we should really try to make friends with as many people as possible and, if possible, making all those friends as Christian ones .

Some people even try to make friends when they are all alone .

The best way to do that each time is to pray because when you might be doing that, God will notice your prayers, and He will come in and answer them and help you out in the best way each time .

As for both friendships and families, we can always get God included into those relationships, and that is the best way to go because it makes those relationships more peaceful and friendly . It's just a great way to combine with those other people in our lives .

We can even bond with other people who are not Christians at this current time, but possibly, after a period of time, we can tell them the information they need to know about God . And if we pray for them, there is a very good chance that those people are going to become Christians in the same way that we are .

With having such good relationships with so many people everywhere we go, we can really live up a life, but the main thing we need to keep in our minds is having a strong and stable relationship with God at all times .

He helps us through everything and shows us the way to live our lives in the proper ways, so we should definitely be following Him throughout our lives . By doing that, we will have more peaceful lives and also more of a chance at profitable lives .

Profitable lives are good for everyone, but not everyone has the opportunity to get that chance . There are a lot of people who are living on the streets these days, and they ask everybody who passes by them for money . Giving those people a bit of money is a good way of showing some of God's love toward them .

Another way to think of God is like this . He is like a bank . When we are going through any hard times in our lives, we can take those things and pray about them so those things will be deposited into that bank, but we don't have to worry because God answers those prayers and sends messages at times .

With God doing that, we can definitely think of Him as the best banker that we have ever had . We can do that because He is probably depositing those things, with us, into heaven when we die, but I think that He would do that closer to the time that we prayed those prayers .

A love life is also really important to every person these days, and the one for everyone who they can all make that type of a relationship with is God . He is definitely the best one to do that with because He created love .

CHAPTER 8

Grasp His Hands and Let Him Lead

As was said in the title of the book, God Is the Man, Take His Hands, we should take God by His hands when He comes in to help us and to show His love and to teach us all those different helpful lessons to be led down the proper road to the destination we are trying to reach at that time .

It's not every time that people have to pray first to God to make sure that we are going to be led by Him in the proper manner that we need to be led . Being led by God is the absolute best way to lead in your life because He has the best plans planned out for everyone .

Think of Him in this matter like a tour guide . With tour guides, we sometimes have to take one of their hands to be guided to the place where we aim to get to . It's not just God, Jesus, and the Holy Spirit who do that, but they sometimes send out angels who have been taught in the appropriate ways that they are supposed to do their duties .

We can also do some touring ourselves . At times, God might come and send us a message that tells us to spread the information about Him to the people who don't know about Him yet . By doing that, it will help to make those people's lives better than what they are like right now .

Touring times are great times to stabilize our relationships with our families and friends, so that will definitely make our lives much more peaceful . Having peaceful times in between people is the best way for anyone's relationships to be built .

To build a good and stable relationship with God, Jesus, and the Holy Spirit, the main things we should be doing are these things:

1. Going to the church services on Sunday morning or in the evening

2. Praying to get into good communication with them

3. Taking the things that we learn at the church services seriously and live them out fully in our lives

Now, with God being like a doctor, we can be fully sure all the time that He will heal us up when we pray to Him or when other people pray for us about those same situations .

And also, when we might pray about others that we hear about or that we know already that need help, there is a very good chance that God is going to come in and help out those people in a loving way .

One of the other ways that God is like a doctor is like this . He gives out advice and suggestions for everything we are doing in our lives these days . He tells us to do things in ways that will not just help us out in better ways, but those suggestions will also help out other people in really good ways also .

So helping out as many people as we possibly can in helpful ways is a good thing to do because giving out that help to as many people as possible is something that God is definitely telling us to do with our lives .

There are so many different ways to help others out these days, so if you really want to help any of those other people are living all around the world right now, the main thing to do for them is to pray for them and maybe even send some donations . Those donations can be done with the Salvation Army and other companies like that one . Now, just think about how many people you might have possibly helped out at that time . The higher the amount, the better .

The sad thing, though, is that there is such a high number of people who are really needing help in all parts of their lives . What we all should do is help those people out in whatever way that we can and maybe even make some small friendships with some of them, which, you might not believe, can actually work out in people's lives .

By taking God by His hands and letting Him lead you to whatever destination you may be headed, you will definitely have calmer travels in that status .

Everybody likes to have a nice, calm life to live each day, but the only problem is that Satan gets into our lives at times and raises up some turbulence . When Satan does that in our lives, we just need to remember to deeply pray about that over and over again until the situations have been defeated by the works that God has been doing for us .

And then we definitely need to give thanks to God for helping us out in that loving way each time . There is absolutely no one better than God who can do that type of stuff, so take His hands .

GOD WILL HOLD YOUR HANDS

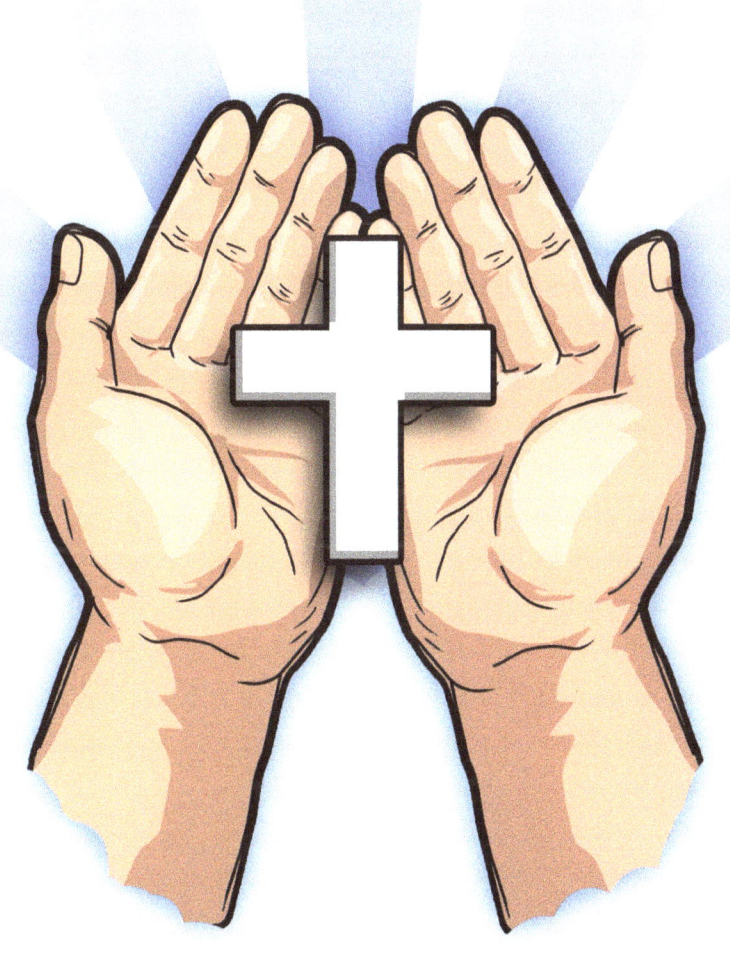

CHAPTER 1

God Is Always There

The world has so many different gods which any person can choose from any day, but the one thing that everyone needs to realize is that the only god that is actually a true god is the Christian God .

The reason why I say that is because I'm supposed to be dead right now from a car accident that happened back when I was thirteen years old . I never had anything to worry about, though, because the entire time I was dead, my mother was praying for me, and God came to me with the doctors and brought me back to life again .

Being a Christian and worshipping our God is the absolute best thing that anyone can do these days . The reason for that is because with us being in the family of God, everything is so peaceful and easy .

No matter what incident a person might get into these days, God will always be there to back them up . All they need to do is to go to Him in prayer and ask for His help . It doesn't matter what they might be needing the help for, but God loves everyone so much, He will help us all out for anything because He is our loving father .

If you want to get associated with a group of people who meet every week for a prayer group time, you should check at your church to see if they have one there . If they don't have one there yet, suggest to them to start one up and tell them that the reason is because God always comes through with helping His children .

Anything that any person does in these current days can be really confusing . Those are things like medications, or if you are in a class, or the information to do with a person's bank accounts, etc .

Any of those selections of confusion are obviously not helpful to any person's life unless they want to live their life in a bit of a comical way, which can turn out to be a rather profitable life to live .

To get out of that confusion, just follow God . To follow God, go to church services on Sundays, learn more about Him there, and also worship Him . Being in a church is a great place to make friends with other people who are Christians .

So I guess we can say that God is the absolute best therapist that anyone can ever get anywhere on the world right now, so everybody just needs to take as much as we can out of the situation to keep things working .

The reason why God is such a good therapist is because when we pray to Him for help, and if any of those prayers have mental reasons in them, God will help us out in the perfect way we need to be helped at that particular time .

We can use that therapy whenever we want to by praying to Him and asking Him for His assistance in the situation we might be in at that time . God is the absolute best "therapeutic doctor" that anyone can find anywhere .

There are so many different religions all around the world right now . The amount and different types of religions do attract many different people, but the thing is that God wants everyone to be a part of His family, but it is a choice that everyone has to make for themselves .

We just need to accept the meanings from the Christian religion and try to spread it around to as many friends and family as possible . Doing that is a great thing to do because picture in your mind the heavenly place where we will be sent to when we die . It's a true reward .

There are so many places in the world that need help right now financially, medically, and many other ways as well . But the main help they all need is to be led to believe in God and to become Christians .

There are also all sorts of different wars happening all over the world right now . Those wars are between countries, companies, illegal drugs, religions, etc . These wars can be so damaging to our children, but some people get involved in some of those wars, and they don't know that information .

Even though we have all these different wars, God will always guide us to the proper way we need to go because He loves us so much . God is also the strongest warrior fighting in all the wars we are fighting in these days, and if we are in His team during the wars, we won't have much to worry about because 90 percent of the time, He defeats Satan, no matter what Satan is trying to do .

With having the knowledge that God is here with us, our lives can be much easier to live than usual . Having God in our lives is a blessing that can never be beaten because throughout our lives, He will guide and helps us in whichever way He sees is the best way for us at that time .

We all just really need to remember to follow the rules God has laid out for everyone to obey . The only problem is, though, that everybody hears the messages from God, but so many people just seem to rebel against God and everything He is teaching to us . They need to be told that God is the one and only way to choose when any person is making a decision for a religion .

God is like a teacher . He is that way because He helps all of us out so much in so many different ways . He even teaches us the basics about how to be a Christian and also the ways in which we need to work with other people to survive in the world these days .

Being taught by a teacher like God is a true blessing that everyone has the chance to take the advantage of . All we need to do is start going to church services on Sundays where we can learn more about God and Jesus and the Holy Spirit, which help us to strongly grow in the direction God wants us to grow in our life .

God is not just a teacher, but He is also a very loving Father who loves every person who is alive at this current time right now . Any person can become a member of Gods' family, and when they do that, it's like a big party starts and continues for the rest of their lives .

We must help other people realize how they need to become a part of God's family in order to live the form of a life that God has prepared for you in the best ways .

CHAPTER 2

Go the Golden Way That God Wants You to Go

The fathers who we have here with us on earth right now love us and want the best for us, but the one Father whom we all share, God, loves everybody the same way and only wants the best for everyone .

There is a path that we need to follow to build a stronger relationship with God . We can do that by studying the Bible each day and also praying and getting into good contact with God every day . Having a relationship like that with the Lord is something that everybody should have, but so many people just won't accept it .

The Golden Way that God wants everyone to go these days is that He wants everyone to become a Christian . Being a Christian is very rewarding . It is so rewarding that with the way that God shows His love to everyone, they can easily spread that information to other people who may not know anything about God yet and help them to hopefully become a Christian .

One thing that really needs to be done for all other people who are not Christians is that we need to pray for them . We need to ask God that those people will open their minds and possibly accept Jesus as their Savior . Living a life as a Christian is much more peaceful and calmer in some ways, but not in all ways .

Earlier, I said how God is like a teacher, but He is also like a doctor . The reason why I believe He is like a doctor is because when we pray to Him and request a healing, He blesses us with a healing for whoever may need it at that time, and it doesn't matter what kind of medical problem the person might have, but God loves everyone so much since He is our original Father, and nothing can stop His love .

To get the information about God, the Word, spread to as many other people that you possibly can, this is one of the things that you can do . There is a group called Youth With A Mission (YWAM), and they have bases located all around the world .

At those bases, a person can take a course called Discipleship Training School (DTS) . The DTS is about three months long, and after a person finishes the class, the people go on a three-month outreach to either a different place in their country or a city in different country .

Of the entire time of the outreach, they will be spreading the Word of God to a countless amount of people in whatever area of the world they might be in . They will always be in a team wherever they have been placed, and they all work great together as a team when they are spreading the Word of God to the people who just are so deeply in need of God's love and care in their lives .

There is also the option of the Salvation Army . The Salvation Army is similar to YWAM, but different in many ways, like they have stores that sell things at affordable prices even for people who live on the streets . In those stores they sell clothing, food, books, art, furniture, etc . God has truly blessed North America with the Salvation Army with the way that it always helps all people out in so many ways .

The Salvation Army (SA) has a countless number of churches located all around the world where anyone can attend the services on Sunday mornings . Their churches have youth groups, Bible studies, and other such things where people learn more about God and also have the chance to make friends with other people who attend the church .

The SA also does fundraising for the people who are living in areas who are low on money and food and anything else they might need at that current time . This is one of the ways in which they do it . When Christmastime comes around, they bring out red kettles with bells to ring . The donations are placed directly into the kettle by the pedestrians themselves . They do that so they know that they are making a change in the city at this time .

It's just making the decision between YWAM and the Salvation Army which might be the best way to help other people of the world and also to get the Word of God known by as many as possible in all areas of the world that can be reached at any time .

We are all God's children, but it's up to us if we are going to stay as a part of that family . To do that, all we need to do is become a Christian and find a church where we understand the sermons nice and easily . The more that we can understand what God is teaching us, the better since He is the best teacher on this planet . The information we get from Him will also reward us through our entire life because it will be helping us to build a closer relationship with God .

The same as I said about the Salvation Army's church, churches are a very good place for making friends and getting into groups that might meet two times a month or more for things like Bible study, music practice, etc . When those groups get together, they bond so well that a lot of those people make friends with each other very easily because they are being led by God .

CHAPTER 3

Let Him Lead You Down the Path You Are on Right Now

God's hands are always open to accept everyone else's hands into His hands . That means that with our hands, we need to try as hard as we can to lead other people to turn away from following the sinful ways that Satan is trying to trick all into turning our backs on God . But those of us who are stable with God will be able to stay with God through everything because He stays with us through all things that might happen in our lives .

One way to think of how God works while He is helping us find our ways down all the different paths we need to deal with through our lives is like this . God is like a map . It doesn't matter where we might pray from or what we may be praying about because God answers prayers that He finds are clean of sin .

We can make sure that our prayers are going to be free of sin when we pray them to God by doing this . Before actually praying, we are supposed to ask God to forgive us of any sins we may have committed in the past .

For those of us who have progressed to either side of this Holy War we all are in every day of our lives, we all need to remember that our lives are not just going to be stressful in the usual physical ways, but also stressful at times in spiritual ways too .

We don't have much to worry about, though, about the way in which the Holy War has a spiritual side to it . God and Satan are always fighting against each other, and sad to say, not all of us are on God's side right now, so that makes it into a true Spiritual War being fought by all three parties—mankind, God, and Satan .

In the beginning of every person's life, no one can tell what type of a life they are going to be living out . A lot of people were taken to church when they were children, but it's hard to say what happened in their life, so a percentage of those people may have decided not to become a Christian and just live their life in a more worldly or secular way .

With all those things happening in people's lives these days, it is hard to figure out the direction of which way our lives are going to be headed .

Those directions are our choices, like the good side with God or the evil side with Satan . When the majority of people hear about Satan, they do not want to have anything to do with Satan and all his evil plans he has going on all around the world twenty-four hours a day of every year .

That just proves how much better God's side is in this situation because good is always better than evil, so with God being good, He will always be superior above Satan, who is evil . God is also with us twenty-four hours a day, every month of every year .

CHAPTER 4

Join God's Family, It's a Great Party!

God's family starts out with three in it—God, Jesus, and the Holy Spirit—but at any time, we may decide to, we can join that family for the rest of our lives and also all eternity .

We all have our families with us here on earth, which we were born with, but there are some people who have been left to raise themselves and hopefully find a job that will help them to get through all that financial stress that is in everybody's lives these days .

There is so much that is needed to be done all around the world right now to get the information about God to be heard by as many people as possible . A lot of people, after they have heard that info the first time, will probably try out a church service one Sunday morning, and a lot of those people are probably going to become a Christian or, in other words, join up with God's family .

Helping other people to become a member of God's family is something great to do because we just mainly need to aim at helping out anyone at any time anywhere so everybody will have the chance of becoming a Christian soon .

There are so many different religions all around the world right now for people to choose from, but with the status that Christianity has, the basic person would probably make the choice of being a Christian because it is much more peaceful than all the other religions the world has to offer at this time . Going to a Christian church on a Sunday for a church service to learn more about God and the way in which He runs His religion of Christianity is something that is really good to do for any person of any age because bonding with God is like winning a billion dollars, but no price can ever be put on Him .

Those of us who have already become a member of God's family, we can really help out anyone else by just asking God to lead us in the direction that is going to help us out the best at that time and also for the rest of our lives .

It's not just ourselves that we need to focus on all the time, but we also have to help out all those people who are living all around the world right now to get to know God and to make the correct choice to turn away from Satan and to accept God as their leader for the rest of their life .

When a person becomes a Christian, God is so happy and loving to everyone, so that just makes that time a time every person would want to experience for their entire life .

When you are a part of God's family and if you have gotten together with a group of other people you know from church to join up with a Bible Study group, it's a great way to make friends and also to have pure parties .

CHAPTER 5

God Is the Sunshine in Our Lives

God loves everyone who is living right now and everyone who has ever lived in the entire history of mankind, and this makes Him like the large, warm, full sun that gives all of us heat and definite help with everything we need in our lives . With God guiding us every day, there is just absolutely no other way that can be found that is as good as God .

One of the ways in which God is the sunshine in our lives is that whenever we are trying to bond with any other people, we have the backup of God to help us through any situation we might be going through at any time in our lives .

A person's life may be confusing, but when they ask God for help in that situation, no matter what the situation might be, He will come at a time and help them out in the way in which He sees is the best way for them to be helped at that time . When He does that, it is just a full way of Him showing His full love to the person whom He is assisting at that current time .

With God being the sunshine in our lives, that must mean that Satan is the dark evening sky, but both of them are actually around us all the time every day, week, and year long, but it just comes up to us to make to proper choice on which one of them we are going to choose because the choice will either send us to hell or to heaven . Just learn and try to listen to God .

With Satan being the darkness like that, that means he is creating darkness in everyone's lives and trying as hard as he can to make all our lives as horrid as possible to live, but we just need to remember that God is with us, helping us through the entire way .

Yes, God is with everyone all the time, but there are a lot of people who have been taken in by the temptation coming from Satan . Those people spread that information around to the rest of mankind, hoping to get some of them either fully Christian or made into Satanists .

Even though God might be with everyone at all time of their lives when they need to be assisted, not all people are going to feel like He is fully helping at all times, but they just need to realize that God will hold your hand and guide you through any stressful times you might go through .

The best thing to do for any person is just to reach out with one of their hands and take a good grip of one of God's hands, maybe have a really good handshake with Him . You never know, you might be able to get into a really good conversation, but the main thing is that it will all be done in prayer .

What we need to do is to spread that sunshine God is shining on us to all the people who we may know or may meet who are not Christians to hopefully give them the full option of whether or not they want to become a Christian or just stay the way that they are at that time .

It never really matters what any person might pray about or what they might do; every person sins during their lifetime . It's just up to us in the end to make the correct decision about if they are going to stay with God for the rest of their life or if they are going to turn and head toward the evilness Satan is trying to tempt everyone with .

The Lord is much more powerful than we are, and He is also

more powerful than how Satan is, but the only thing is that to get God overpowering Satan, we really need to pray hard because Satan does his work in serious/hard ways .

No matter what Satan might be trying to do anywhere around the world, God will always be by our sides . All we need to do is just show that we are fully on His side and willing to do whatever He asks us to do at any time .

GOD IS THE WORLD'S BEST DOCTOR

CHAPTER 1

Just One Doctor for All the Sinful Illnesses

Ever since birth, we have been receiving both the spiritual and physical help from God, which every person on this planet needs desperately at this time . The reason for that is because of the things that are occurring in the world at this time, both physical and spiritual, and those things are doing nothing but damage to us in horrific ways .

Those damaging evil ways Satan has invented can be stopped by praying to God and asking Him for His aid in those circumstances . We don't need to fear that much because God is superior to everything that Satan is trying to do . The main problem is that Satan doesn't realize that .

Without Satan knowing that God is superior to him in all things, that just makes Satan much easier to defeat in any way . It just mainly depends on if we are praying about it when we or others are needing the help to get away from Satan and all his evil .

Keeping close to God because of the sins we committed, they will stay with us unless we ask God to forgive us for those sins we have committed .

So many of the television shows these days are just filled with details on murders, and they also have lots of swearing in them . A lot of people who watch those types of shows, unfortunately, their lives change to run in a similar way those shows' storylines run each time . There are also a lot of other shows centered around sexual detail, which is definitely not good for people of young age, and we have to protect their innocence .

Pornography is accepted by too large of an amount of people these days that it can just really make people not realize that pornography is truly something Satan created to take us away from the arms of God by sinning in that manner . It is fully our own choice if we decide to get into the porno way of sinning or just to keep ourselves fully out of it in all ways and just to follow God and His teachings .

All in all, following God is something we all are allowed to do, but the people around us just might not care for that these days and could be going for something completely opposite to that group of things to do in our lives these days besides worshipping God as much as we can .

CHAPTER 2

Beat the Sins with a Big Grin!

There is a countless amount of sinful illnesses these days that are all very hard to deal with if you don't ask God for His spiritual help, which He gives out in a loving way to everyone .

Here is a description of the sinful illnesses:

1. Swear words, both verbal and in writing

2. Murdering other people

3. Stealing—A lot of people these days feel like they need to steal from all things right now to survive in their lives with the way the world is running right now

Situations arise that make people feel like they have to swear in a very loud and evil-sounding way, so it is just easy to tell that Satan has invented these sins . Anything that can pull us away from God is like a rope that Satan is holding in his hands and has tied around our waists, and he is trying hard all the time to pull us toward everything he has created in the world right now .

That is a serious sinful illness, and with God as our doctor, we just need to pray to Him and ask Him for His help in that matter, and if I'm right, He will cut those ropes Satan has tied around us and anyone else who we might be praying for .

It never matters how many times a person might sin in a day because if they go to God in prayer and ask Him to forgive them of their sins, there should be no doubt in their minds that He is going to do that because He is everyone's most loving father that there has ever been in anyone's family line .

Most people think that all things that have to do with Satan are going to overpower God and then take full control of earth, but that is fully not true because God cannot be overpowered by anything . I'm just wondering why Satan doesn't know that information yet after all these years of fighting against God .

Those people who think in those positive ways about Satan are definitely going to go to hell and be tortured for eternity when they die, or they can decide to follow God and get to know Him better before they die because God is a leader giving out love and care every moment of every day . It's everybody's final choice to make in this situation, and hopefully, they will choose the one that is going to give them a very pleasurable payback .

Sinning is not a way of saying thank you to the Lord for all the great things He has done for you throughout your life so far . If you are really wanting to express to other people how thankful you are for God's care and love, then start doing things for others to help them out in the areas that they are in need of help .

There are people in every city and town all around the world these days who are in need of help from other people in the ways of financial and food and many other ways too . If we just keep helping in the areas that we are able to, things will get better for those people and hopefully lead a good amount of people toward becoming Christians .

CHAPTER 3

God's Word Is Meant to Be Heard

Getting with a group like the Salvation Army is a great way to get the assistance that you might need at that time to help you with getting the food, clothing, and other things you may be in need of at that time, and they can also show an awesome way to spread the Word of God around the area of the city you are living in at that time .

There are quite a few other groups of Christians that get together in areas, and they get taught like this . This one has the name of YWAM, which stands for Youth With A Mission, and they have bases worldwide . Any person who is a Christian can sign up for a DTS, which is a Discipleship Training School course, and after you get trained, you go on an outreach for a while with the other people who were in your course to either somewhere nearby or another place in the world .

I was with my parents when they took their training with YWAM, and then did the outreach back in 1989–1990 . On that outreach, the group went to what was the biggest city in Malaysia at that time, and some of our group stayed there to do some spreading of God's information while the rest of us went to Bangkok in Thailand, and we spent about three months going all around Thailand spreading God's Word to as many people as we could, and our team reached over one thousand in the jungles and the cities and towns .

Getting out into the jungles at the young age that I was back then and telling those people about God was just great because the way that the team had the ones my age doing it was to do acting performances that were fully understood and accepted by the people there . Because we did those performances for them, such a large amount of those people realized that God was calling them to join in with Him in His family, and a large portion of them did accept Jesus into their hearts as their Savior, which is the truthful way to live a life .

I have taken my own DTS with YWAM in a town named Melbourne, which is in Australia . I made a lot of friends while doing that course, and I also learned a lot of really helpful information for sharing details about Christianity and its creator, God, mainly for when we go on our outreach after we finish the course, and our outreach was at the Olympics held in Sydney, Australia, in 2000 .

We got to make signs that portrayed Christian messages to the other people reading them, and we carried them in the opening ceremony march the Olympics was having at the beginning of their show . Our signs were fully accepted by everyone .

If that can be fully accepted by so many people these days, both Christian and also people who might follow other religions or no religion at all, it spreads the information around to everyone who doesn't know it fully yet or even just the basics of it to fill people's minds with questions for themselves, like "Should I try out a church this Sunday?"

It's hard to say how those people are going to answer that question . It is just fully a personal decision every person is having to make when they first hear or read or get told that message . All things are getting more difficult these current days, so we just have to find a way to live through, and the best way is God .

CHAPTER 4

God Is the Man, so Take His Hands

To every person who is alive right now, God is their father, and He will be with them for eternity . That time period includes from the day that they become a Christian here on earth, and then living out through the rest of their life, hopefully as a Christian focused on living by the rules God has made for everyone to follow through their lives .

When anyone prays to God, the first thing they should do in that time of prayer is ask God to forgive them for their sins they have committed because then they will be closer to God by being clean of those sins, and they will be able to hold on to one of God's hands and go on a lifelong journey with Him, which can only go bad if we turn away from Christianity in any way during that journey .

So many people these days think that with the ways that Christianity is being used in television shows and in movies, it is making them think that Christianity is not real . They are actually thinking that it's just a big joke that someone thought up at one moment . We all know, though, that God is real, and He never lets people down . He always comes through for them when He says, in His ways, that He is going to help out in that situation .

We need to get out into our neighborhoods and spread the information about God, as good as we know Him, to as many other people as we possibly can whenever we have the open time to do that . We must think of ourselves like the neighborhood "newspaper" being delivered to everyone at that time when we are spreading that information . It's actually a good thing to picture yourself as if you are keeping a good, strong focus on God to keep a solid relationship with Him right now and also until you die .

Even teenagers these days participate in doing things like that . That may not sound believable, but a lot of teens are actually strong Christians and have built themselves a really good, strong relationship with God and are going to continue with that throughout the rest of their lives since they began it back at such a young age .

The teens go to youth groups, which are held in churches, and they meet up with friends, and they also get taught a lot of information about being a Christian from the leader of their group who gives little sermons to them, which they like to listen to .

As those kids get older, they get hit by all the things that are happening in the world these days that really give a chance of messing up their lives . Some of them turn away from being a Christian by the age of eighteen, but a lot of them stay stable in their faith in God, which will definitely help them through their lives .

Anybody getting help to fully understand the details about Christianity before they make a full decision is something that truly needs to be done . That is why I was in YWAM . I am also doing things as much as I can with the Salvation Army, which does similar things, but it definitely spreads God's Word to people of any age or race in any place they might be .

All in all, staying with your Father God during the walk of your lifetime is due to be thought as a true bonding and searching time between you and God, who loves all .

CHAPTER 5

Who Is Alive?

People get asked all different kinds of questions these days, and of course, when someone asks you a question, they are usually expecting you to answer it . One of the questions could be this one: "Who do you know that is alive?" You can answer them in so many different ways because there is just an endless amount of names being used all around the world these days .

That question can also be answered by saying "God" because He is alive and will never leave us because we are a part of His family, and He shows us and everyone else so much love and care all the time .

There is absolutely no way to question the detail that God is alive because He is healing people all the time in prayer sessions and also getting them more money and food and things like those and plenty of other things people everywhere need at this current time .

If you compare your thoughts of those things to your thoughts of what is medically happening in the world these days, it can really make God seem like a doctor to you, which is a very good aspect to have of Him because doctors these days are more helpful than you might know of because there is a larger amount of different kinds of doctors then what you actually know of, and God can heal anything .

God is the best in any form of a working chain because He is the one with the power to change anything that is happening in any area of the world at any time . We should all be very thankful for that since so much in the world needs to be changed each day because the world is really getting messed up a lot every day, and that is definitely not good for anyone's lives .

Some ways to get fully informed on the details of Christianity is to listen to Christian radio stations or to go to Christian sites on the internet and read books that are Christian and also watch TV shows that are Christian based .

One way to know that God and the other two are alive all the time is by really doing some more of a deeper study into Christmas and also Easter because they both hold deep detail to the life of Jesus and how that affects all of us and how much God helps us out all the time, whether we ask for His help or not, due to His love and care that He is holding for everyone and also everything .

We are very lucky that He cares about everything happening in the world right now, and with that care that He has, He will help us to defeat Satan in any battle that we have to fight against him .

It seems like everybody is thinking that evil is running the world these days, but the truth that they need to know and accept is that the good and bad/evil are at a constant war right now, and the only way to defeat Satan and his evil warriors is to fight in that battle with God as one of His warriors who are armored with goodness .

GOD CALLS ON US EVERYDAY!

CHAPTER 1

It's Like He's Using a Microphone

Everybody's ears are wide open for the messages that God is going to be sending to them, but unfortunately, their ears are also taking in messages from Satan to attract everyone toward him and to fully forget the details about God .

It's just up to each person to make their own choice of whether or not they are going to follow God or go the other way and follow Satan . Following either of them can be confusing, but if you are thinking about following God, then go to a church service one Sunday morning or evening and join in with what is being done at that time and listen to the sermon that the pastor gives out during the service .

During a church service, a lot of things can be done during those times, like making friends, and you could get into a Bible study group that is in your area of the town you live, and when you are going to that, you will build a much stronger connection with God than you had before .

The way in which it's like God is using a microphone is because He speaks to either just one person at a time or a group at a time, or you never know He might decide to talk to all the people who are living right now, so they have the chance of making the proper decision or going the other way .

When a person prays to God, there are so many different ways He has to choose from to fully communicate with any person who may be praying to Him at that time . People can pray for anything that might be causing some kind of turbulence in their lives or maybe just wanting to help other people out in the best way that they ever possibly can .

When God is using His "microphone," the messages He is sending out to all of us are being sent by worldwide speakers, so everyone will have the opportunity to hear all His information . Any person can take that info and use it in their life any way that they want to, but they should ask God which way that they should use it because His directions always guide the people who are using it to the correct destination .

A lot of us are those "speakers" that God uses for His "microphones ." He has chosen humans to be the ones who spread all the information He wants to share with everyone all around the world right now because we listen to each other and also help out each other in the best ways that we can .

When that information gets spread around the area we might be in at that time, it can turn out to be very helpful for whoever we might have helped during that time .

The Salvation Army spreads all the info God has to offer every day, and they will help out anyone who wants to get closer to God or even people who just have questions about that situation . All in all they are a great group to get with, and they have churches too .

In the end, it's just up to each person to make their own personal choice of what they are going to do at that point in their life, but the main decision is whether or not they are going to follow God or follow Satan . Hopefully, everyone will decide to follow God because He is the one who replenishes our lives when we are in need, and He aids us when we might be needing any kind of help .

CHAPTER 2

God Is the Man, Just Take His Hands

God is the leader for a lot of people who are living these days, but the only problem is that some of those people aren't fully informed about God and what He does for everyone each day of their lives .

God is very loving, attractive to most people, but there are other religions that say that their gods are loving also, but the only thing is that those other religions are all led by Satan, but he goes by other names in most of them .

Gripping onto one of God's hands and allowing Him to lead you to all through your life and also make your choices for you will be a much better decision for anyone these days with the way the world is running right now .

When any person has such a good connection with God like that one, they shouldn't just think about themselves, but they should also keep other people in their minds and mainly what they should help them with at that time .

Reading the Bible can be like holding His hands because we get great guidance from the scriptures that He blesses us with at times during our prayer times and also in church services . God put those scriptures into the Bible to teach everyone the things they need to be taught and also to bring them closer to God and other members of His family .

God is the one, even for the fun! That saying is true because people are born because He created mankind, and He also brings us together to marry each other in weddings and show love to each other the same way He shows it to all of us . To say it in an easy way, God is everyone's leader; the only thing is, though, that not every person actually decides to learn about Him and follow in His way (e .g ., become a Christian), which is a very good decision for anyone to make during their life .

The information about God that we can give out to other people each day is like handing out wrapped gifts . Those gifts have been wrapped by God's hands, and we don't have anything to worry about because He always finds the absolute best place to get them from, and that place is the same place each time—His love-filled heart .

God at times can be like one of those boxes a person sends parcels to other people through the mail, but when God gets delivered to each of us, it's hard to say at times what we are going to be receiving from that magnificent package .

Even though we all should be so thankful each day because of the things that God does for everyone, there are so many people who do not even acknowledge that He is here with us all every day of our lives .

A lot of those people who have decided not to be with God are automatically with Satan because Satan's side is the only other side that there is besides God's side in the world of religions .

Isn't it a bit too harsh for those people that they haven't being getting the help that they need? But that is probably because they are following Satan at that time and haven't heard the truth about God yet . When a person becomes a Christian, they should spread the info about God when they are feeling calm with doing that . It helps other people so much in their own lives and has a very good chance in making good friendships .

CHAPTER 3

Where Is God Calling You to Go?

When you go to church services or Bible studies or other things like those you can get a lot of prayer in, ask God where He wants you to go start up as a missionary or to join in with a missionary group to spread His Word .

I have joined up with a couple of missionary groups, and these are their names: Youth With A Mission (YWAM), which is a worldwide Christian missionary organization, and the other group's name is the Salvation Army, which spreads the Word of God also and helps out people with getting food and clothing and whatever things they need .

When I was just about nine or ten years old, my parents took me and my sister to the head base of YWAM, which is on the big Hawaii island, the city of Kona . After my parents had finished their training with YWAM, which is called a Discipleship Training School (DTS), we, including the people who were in that class with them and their children, all left on an outreach to a couple of countries in Asia . The countries we went to were Thailand and Malaysia .

When our group first arrived over in that area, we were in the city of Singapore, which is in Malaysia . Our group then split into two groups . The group that we were in the next day or two headed to a YWAM base in a city in Thailand and started spreading the Word of God as best as we possibly could to as many people that we might get into contact with .

In Thailand, we even got to go to the jungles and some of the villages where people were living, and when we got to those villages, we told them about God and cooked them a bit of our kind of food, and those of us who were around my age back then (1989–1990), we played with the kids whose homes were in those places, and we also told them where to go if they had any questions about why all of us had come to their place .

At that age, I wasn't one for holding in Asian food, but they did make it good, even though it has never been similar to the type of food that we eat here over in North America . There were some differences between the food a person could get in a restaurant and the other ones they would get in those villages . In the villages, we were served raw chicken feet at one village . For breakfast they made us chicken, rice and garlic porridge for an early morning breakfast . For other meals, they served us boa constrictor, and sometimes we would get rattlesnake, and with the rattlesnake, we would use it like bacon because when they would cook it over their huge bonfire, it actually came out tasting delicious .

All in all, it can take a different amount of time for everyone to decide what they are going to do with their life, but if they feel any kind of calling coming from God telling them what to do with their lives, they just need to focus on that topic a bit harder, which is like telling God that they are fully aimed at hitting the target He has made for them to hit .

It doesn't matter where God tells you to go to, but we all need to remember this . Wherever God sends you, keep your heart fully open to help as many other people in whatever ways as possible .

With that fully open heart in you, love is automatically one of the first things to be dispensed from it . The love in your heart has been blessed from the heart and hands of God .

God loves every person, and He forgives all sins, so every person has a really good chance at making a good relationship with Him, and in becoming a full Christian, it all just depends on which way the person decides they want their own personal spiritual life to run, either with God or Satan .

CHAPTER 4

Helping Others Can Be a Bother, but God Will Fix That Situation

Times come up when your neighbors or strangers might really be in need of help . There are also a lot of people these days who are living on the streets who are very poor and in need of assistance .

Some churches make groups with other churches, and with those groups, they go out and help out all around in the city they are located in, and they try as hard as they can to help out in the areas in the city that need the help they are able to give to them .

Helping others is like showing love to other people, but you don't need to hold in that love so tightly as you would back when you were a teenager . When you see how much you actually have helped other people, just continue helping in that area so as many people as you are able to reach can be helped at that particular time .

If you know any other people who want to help out other people, see if they would like to join you when you are spreading the Word of God to as many people as you can each day, or maybe just giving out the information about how to follow God these days because with the way that the world is running right now, Christianity has become confusing .

It doesn't ever matter what kind of a situation we might be in, but God will always show us the way to get ourselves out of those situations . Some of those situations can be painful, and other ones can be fun . It's pretty much the same as everything else, but it is hard to tell what's going to happen in one of those situations; so when you need guidance, just pray and ask God for that help .

A large amount of people can be helped these days by donations of money or clothing and food and things like that . Donations of those things can be made at a lot of churches and also at the Salvation Army office, which is in majority of cities these days .

A lot of people use the Salvation Army for when they need things like clothing and canned foods, and the Salvation Army is such a kind and polite group . They are really good to get associated with because if you are looking for a friend, anyone can make good friends there .

God, ever since any person was born, has been wanting to lead them through their lives and show them completely what to do with their lives while they are following Him . And then when a person prays about something, God answers that prayer and shows them that He is with everyone all the time, like when we are needing His compassion, which gives us His love at the same time, and His love will never end .

All in all, helping other people also helps the people who have helped them . If you are wanting to start helping others now, just go through your house and look for canned foods you won't eat and maybe any clothing you need to get rid of that isn't damaged .

Once you have gotten all the things that you want to donate, take them to your church or the local Salvation Army office to make the donation, and then, if you want to, set up a calendar with them for the usual times you will be doing your donations . And there is one other thing to remember: "Share the Word, it's meant to be heard ."

CHAPTER 5

The World Is Running, but Which Way Is It Going?

A lot of the world is just running in a very sinful way . There is still, though, a good amount of us who are running our part of the race and heading straight toward God, and while we are running, we are trying to get other people to join with us on our side of this race .

There are only two sides to this race; one is God's side, and the other side is Satan's side . God's side is full of purity and truth and love and also peace, while Satan's side is full of evilness and hate and distribution of the illegal and deadly things that are bad for any person these days .

Satan is trying so hard every day to get into everyone's lives and make their lives completely horrid . All we need to do is pray to God and ask for His help to defend us from Satan's hits on us, and we don't have anything to worry about because God always comes in those situations and fights off Satan from His children .

God is going all around the world spreading His love and everything else that He is wanting to give out to everyone, but the only thing is that His enemy, Satan, is coming up with new ways to battle Him in those spiritual ways every day . God will never be the loser in one of those battles against Satan because He made everything, including all the angels such as Lucifer, whose name got changed to Satan .

For some people who aren't following any religion, just go around and do whatever is happening in the world at that particular time . It doesn't matter to them what they might be doing or what area they would be in because they don't believe in sin or God or actually any kind of religion . That can be confusing, but it doesn't matter which way your life might be leading you; just remember that God's door is always open for you to enter His Kingdom .

With so many people not knowing where there are going to these days because of either financial or medical reasons, things like those can really make our world into a confusing maze that will take all of us a very long time to get through .

As we travel through that maze, we have a really good map, God, and He will show us the proper directions we need to go while we travel through that confusing path .

When I run in that path, I just want to hit my destination of God's Kingdom . Once I get there, I really want to find out what God wants me to do with my life next . Upon finding out that info, you should write down on a calendar the times that you want to get out, and then get prepared for doing whatever He has set up for you .

People can be helped in any places these days, so when you go out and get into a conversation with a stranger, if the topic comes close enough, bring God into it and tell them the info about God and your church and how God might have helped you earlier in your life .

God helps anyone at any time, but it's just up to each person to set up their own relationship with God on their own so they can bond with Him in a stronger way than by just becoming a Christian back when they were a child .

We all have so much to believe in and so much to fight against; just remember to stay on God's side of this spiritual war because in the book of Revelation in the Bible, God is going to defeat Satan, and all Christians are going to go to heaven when He comes back to earth . It's just hard to say if He is going to be coming in human form or spiritual, but either will be good .